An Insider's Guide to Making School Systems Work

Jorea M. Marple

A ScarecrowEducation Book
Published in partnership with the
American Association of School Administrators

The Scarecrow Press, Inc.
Lanham, Maryland, and Oxford
2002

A ScarecrowEducation Book
Published in partnership with
the American Association of School Administrators

Published in the United States of America
by Scarecrow Press, Inc.
A member of the Roman & Littlefield Publishing Group
4720 Boston Way, Lanham, Maryland 20706
www.scarecroweducation.com

12 Hid's Copse Road
Cumnor Hill, Oxford OX2 9JJ, England

British Library Cataloguing in Publication Information Available

Library of Congress Cataloging-in-Publication Data

Marple, Jorea M., 1949–
    An insider's guide to making school systems work / Jorea M. Marple.
        p. cm.
    Includes bibliographical references (p.) and index.
    ISBN 0-8108-4187-8 (pbk. : alk. paper)
    1. School management and organization—United States.   2. Educational
leadership—United States.   I. Title.

LB2805 .M284   2002
371.2'00973—dc21   2001049347

Contents

Introduction

> ... our education governance system, as currently operating is a serious barrier to improving our schools.
>
> —Committee for Economic Development,
> *Putting Learning First*

> The whole people must take upon themselves the education of the whole people and be willing to bear the expense of it.
>
> —John Adams, President and Statesman, 1785,
> Quoted in Center on National Education Policy,
> *Do We Still Need Public Schools*

An Insider's Guide to Making School Systems Work is a practical guide for operating effective school systems through the establishment of organization, management, and improvement core components designed to reduce the politicized interference in decision-making activities of boards, administrators, educators, service personnel, and the community. Decision-making based on politically popular thought is fostered by lack of commitment by boards, superintendents, employees, and communities to a common focus supported by established core components. Establishing and committing to core organization, management, and improvements components are necessary to overcome political resistance to professional activities and initiatives designed to make school systems work.

Superintendents need to exert the leadership to clearly define personnel and programmatic organizational requirements, a management system, and an improvement process that achieves the board's established vision. Through policy and/or superintendent contract, boards need to commit to support the organization, management, and improvement components set forth by the administration. The lack of definition

1

and commitment to identified components fosters the enhancement of political processes that negatively impact school system success.

Educators are the professionals who need to step forward and clearly assert their expertise in defining the organizational, management, and improvement components necessary for operating effective school systems. The community wants productive schools and a school system, but may not have the sophistication in educational theory, research, and best practice to discern the fundamentals of school system success. Establishing core components for making school systems work takes on the temper of elitism: Without clearly defined minimum personnel and programmatic requirements, management system and improvement process, professional educational activity, and initiatives are often subject to political interference based on populist instincts.

Educators' establishment of minimum organizational requirements, management system, and improvement process shifts a more clearly articulated burden for school system success to boards and community. Boards and the public have become comfortable with blaming educators for students who fail or don't achieve at a given standard. The lack of organized and clearly articulated organization, management, and improvement components has left educators with little recourse but to accept the blame for all public education failures. For too long educators have sent the wrong message to boards and the community, such as that all children—regardless of social, economic, and physical limitations—can obtain the same high level of academic performance even if levies and bonds fail, student-teacher ratios are excessive, teacher pay remains minimal, buildings fail to meet minimum health and safety standards, and inadequate numbers and type of personnel and programs are in place. *An Insider's Guide to Making School Systems Work* establishes the importance of securing a commitment to core components in order to communicate a new message to boards and the community: If minimum organizational requirements are inadequately funded and if management and improvement processes are not supported then less than adequate student performance may occur.

Boards' and communities' commitment and support of organization, management, and improvement components must be linked with strong accountability requirements for administrators and educators in order to achieve a high level of student performance. Unfortunately, accountability for student performance has often been made in isolation, without board and community commitment to defined minimum organizational requirements. For example, educators are held accountable for the performance of "at risk" first-graders who have limited or no readiness activities in the home, no formal preschool education, limited kindergarten instruction, crowded classrooms, no one-on-one reading specialist instruction, and no counseling services. The expectation for "at risk" first-graders to acquire the same level of academic performance as a first-grader from a middle- to upper-class home who has been provided a broad range of readiness activities (music, dance, cultural performances, travel, books, computers, and so on) in the home, preschool instruction, and private tutors and counselors is not reasonable. Educators need to establish minimum personnel and programmatic requirements that will positively affect the "at risk" first-graders' attainment of required reading skills. Minimum requirements such as preschool programs, full-day kindergarten, low student-teacher ratios, and one-on-one reading instruction programs should be established. Board and communities need to understand that without commitment and funding for defined minimum requirements, "at risk" students are less likely to acquire necessary reading skills.

An Insider's Guide to Making School Systems Work provides for the establishment of organization, management, and improvement components that reduce the political rhetoric that interferes with system progress. In too many instances, vision, action, and system improvements are not the determinants of a superintendent's tenure or school system success; rather longevity and outcome are often relegated to the agenda of board members who campaign on what appeals to the underdeveloped political factions in the community. Because board members' agendas are often about political power and control, the system becomes controlled by decisions premised upon anti-intellectual politics and political patronage rather than educational issues and logical process.

Administrators and superintendents are challenged to use their expertise to bring about positive change through cooperative work with the board and involvement of the community. However, the maintenance of an elected board that supports progressive vision over the long term is most unusual. Candidates run for boards with an agenda, and that agenda often includes attacking the professionals leading the system. Attacks on those "in charge" have political appeal. They generally are not based on the "real facts." Tensions between educators, boards, and communities should lessen with initial agreements or understandings between superintendents and boards regarding minimum organizational requirements, management system, system operation, and system improvement.

Developing understanding and commitment in three areas—minimum organizational requirements, an effective management system operation and system improvement process—are the core components for "making school systems work." The recommended components for organization, management, and improvement are based on (1) experiences as a teacher, principal, administrator, and superintendent of schools; (2) analysis of research in management, operation, and instruction; and (3) review of best practices of effective schools and school systems. Educators, administrators, boards, and communities need to have a consolidated focus that is supported by defined organizational requirements, an effective management system, and a comprehensive improvement process.

Commitment to the core components needs to be grounded in an understanding of school system operation. Understanding how school systems operate—and the daily crises, issues, and major tasks they must address—is essential to the development, implementation, and support of core components. Commitment to establish and support minimum organizational requirements, a management system, and an improvement process should be formalized in writing in either or both the superintendent's contract and board policy. A formalized commitment to minimum organizational requirements, a management system, and an improvement process consolidates efforts of boards, superintendent, and employees to make the school system work, for example,keeping the train on the track, laying new track, and keeping peace in the valley. The core components are developed in the following chapters.

Chapter 1 provides the reader with recommendations for minimum organizational requirements in schools and school systems. Based on research and the author's point of view and experience, the recommendations are offered as a starting point for superintendents and board members to arrive at common agreement on minimum organizational requirements for their school district. By agreeing on minimum organizational standards "up front," one can avoid subsequent discussions and confrontations regarding what is important from a specific board member(s)' perspective. Obtaining support for organizational requirements that delineate specific staffing, programs, and services (such as one-to-twelve student-teacher ratio in elementary schools, vice principals for curriculum in secondary schools, and full-day kindergarten instruction) concentrates everyone's focus on achieving requirements, rather than debating their merits in relationship to someone's specific personnel or programmatic desires. Commitment to minimum organization requirements affects both system operation and system improvement, for example, keeping the train on the track, laying new track, and keeping peace in the valley. The recommendations listed in this chapter are designed to generate discussion, development, and commitment from boards, superintendents, and employees to establish minimum organizational requirements for their schools and school district.

Chapter 2 describes a recommended management system that features a high level of accountability. An effective management system is essential for keeping the train on the track, laying new track, and keeping peace in the valley. Successful management systems provide reasonable supervisory ratios to ensure necessary administrative support, frequent monitoring of individual employee and school performance, and increased opportunities to resolve problems at the lowest possible level. Management systems need to define expectations and establish a reporting procedure to measure level of accomplishments. Accountability requirements that hold students, teachers, service personnel, administrators, and board members responsible for their performance as measured against a high standard are fundamental to an effective management system.

Superintendents should carefully define a management system with representative input from the board, employees, and higher education leadership. Boards need to formalize a commitment to the superintendent's management system. The board, administration, and employees should remain committed to a management system as long as demonstrated annual progress is apparent. (Boards' desire to eliminate administrative positions to generate positive political reaction is reduced if boards are required to buy into a management system at the beginning of a new administration.)

Chapter 3 defines a process for bringing about system improvement or "laying new track." This chapter describes elements important to consider in the school and system improvement process, including statistical and factual data for needs assessment, and provides examples of objectives and activities for system improvement in five areas of operation: instruction, communication, finance, operations, and facilities. Examples of anticipated improvements based on defined objectives are listed. Delineating expected improvements or outcomes based on appropriate planning, monitoring, and accountability assists in keeping everyone focused and committed to system improvement efforts.

Chapter 4 discusses school system operation. Understanding what is required just to simply "keep the train on the track" is essential. School systems are complex organizations that require enormous levels of management support just to address daily concerns. In order to keep the system operating, school system administrators daily must face three areas: major tasks, major issues, and daily crises. How a major task or issue becomes a crisis if not properly attended is discussed. Similar tasks, issues, and crises are inherent in the operation of any school system. Lack of understanding of school system operation contributes to public education's low level of credibility and the community's lack of esteem for the system. A well-grounded understanding of school system operations and the daily tasks necessary to "keep the train on the track" is fundamental for those concerned with public education.

Chapter 5 summarizes the core understandings and commitments necessary to make school systems work more effectively. It offers a list of recommendations that need to be understood and supported by boards, superintendent, administrators, teachers, service personnel, and the community.

Educators need to re-assume the leadership role in public education. They need to clearly articulate the minimum organizational requirements—personnel and programmatic—essential in order for all children to attain a high level of achievement and performance. Educators also have a responsibility to establish a management system and an improvement process that result in the efficient daily operation of the school system and ensures student and employee performance as measured against a defined standard. As community representatives, boards need to commit to support and advocate for the core organizational, management, and improvement components for making schools systems work. Educators and boards who demonstrate a unified approach or common focus to establishing and supporting the core components for school system success have a positive impact on the public's perception of school systems. The public's positive perception of school system success equates to more public support and commitment to fund minimum requirements.

Developing these understandings and commitments reduces the political rhetoric that infiltrates all levels of school system operation. With an agreed-on minimum organizational structure, management system, and improvement process, the train remains on the track, new track is laid, and there is greater "peace in the valley."

CHAPTER 1

Minimum Organizational Requirements for Schools and School Systems

Educational leaders must also come to a common understanding of what they believe about school and life in schools, and this activity, too, requires commitment and resources.

—PHILIP C. SCHLECHTY, *INVENTING BETTER SCHOOLS*

Establishment of minimum personnel and programmatic organizational requirements is a core component for making school systems work. Organizational requirements affect all facets of school system operation and success. Organizational requirements enable administrators, employees, and boards to have a common focus and enhance positive working relationships through the reduction of political rhetoric that detracts from professional activity. Organizational requirements for elementary schools, secondary schools, and school systems need to be established and utilized as an essential component for bringing about school and system improvement.

DEFINITION

Minimum organization requirements define personnel and programmatic structures needed to operate effective schools and school systems. Personnel requirements specifically determine the staffing ratios for elementary and secondary schools and the central office, including the number and type of personnel necessary at all levels of operation. Programmatic requirements define the program structures that need to be in place at every level of operation, such as full-day kindergarten, reading recovery, accelerated reading, community service, career clusters, improvement plans, and management plans. The following are examples of basic organizational requirements:

1. *Personnel Requirement: Secondary schools are staffed with one vice principal for every 300 students.* A staffing formula or ratio that determines the number of vice principals assigned to schools is an example of an organizational requirement that needs to be established. The administrative staffing formula should be based on school size and consideration of such variables as percent of at-risk and special needs students. A vice principal ratio should provide necessary support for curricular, administrative, and student issues. It is important that each school district sets a vice principal staffing formula based on its defined criteria.

2. *Personnel Requirement: Elementary and secondary schools are staffed with one counselor for every 250 students.* Counselors are essential positions for all schools, and staffing formulas for counselors should be established as a personnel requirement. Lack of established priority and limited funding have resulted in current national counselor per student ratios of 513:1. A more reasonable counselor/student ratio is 250:1 (American School Counselors Association). Counselor positions are necessary to provide adequate guidance to students on academic, social, and emotional concerns and they constitute an essential element of a basic school structure.

3. *Programmatic Requirement: Full-day kindergarten programs are provided to all students.* Full day-kindergarten is a basic programmatic requirement for elementary schools. Half-day kindergarten models provide less instructional time and are less successful in achieving an adequate readiness level for first grade students.

    Personnel Requirement: Full-day kindergarten programs are staffed with one teacher and one aide for every twenty students. Full-day kindergarten extends learning opportunities and time on task for students; its value has been validated by research and national reform studies.

4. *Programmatic Requirement: One-to-one remedial instruction is provided on a daily basis to first-grade students with skill deficiencies.* Programmatic requirements need to provide first-grade students who are not acquiring necessary reading skills the opportunity to receive one-to-one instruction. A program such as Reading Recovery, that is designed to assist first- and second-grade students acquire necessary reading skills and has an organized accountability structure, provides the necessary one-to-one instruction. Modification of such programs as Title I to provide

one on one instruction should be used to address this programmatic requirement.

Personnel Requirement: All elementary schools are staffed with a reading teacher for every 250 students. Personnel requirements should establish adequate staffing of reading teachers to provide the necessary one-to-one instruction in the primary grades. Reading teacher staffing ratios should consider the percent of at-risk students in each school.

5. *Programmatic Requirement: All high school students must complete at least thirty-two hours of community service each school year.* An expectation that all high school students complete community service hours needs to be a programmatic requirement. Developing a structure that provides opportunities for students to give back to a community that supports public education is valuable for a number of reasons: Students garner an appreciation of the needs of others; students are better able to put their own pressing social and emotional problems in context of others with greater needs; and students are able to enhance positive communication with various entities of the community.

Minimum of personnel and programmatic organizational requirements, such as the examples discussed above, need to be determined by individual school systems. Establishing an agreed-upon listing of minimum organizational requirements limits the board's rhetorical debate. Once requirements are approved, board members should serve as knowledgeable supporters of organizational requirements and provide leadership in advocating for appropriate funding.

PURPOSE

The purpose of developing minimum organizational requirements in each school district is multifold:

- Restore to educators the responsibility of determining minimal organizational requirements;
- Assign to board members the responsibility of understanding the minimum requirements necessary to operate successful schools and school systems;
- Obtain commitment from board members to support, seek funds, and fund minimum requirements;
- Serve as standard to measure what exists against what should exist; and

- Secure common agreement and focus among all constituent groups: teachers, administrators, service personnel, community members, and board members, as to what should be in place in order to make schools and school systems work.

Basic organizational requirements must establish reasonable staff ratios and effective program structures for all levels of operation. Personnel requirements establish basic administrative positions needed in schools and at the system level. Reasonable administrative support and management is essential to effective school system operation, just as it is to a profitable business or industry. In an era of administrator-bashing, it is prudent to establish and obtain support for adequate administrative organization.

Accountability is an important element of any operation that strives to achieve positive results. To achieve these results, accountability requires a reasonable range of supervision. In education, the average number of employees that each administrator supervises is among the highest of any industry or business in America. Personnel requirements need to provide for appropriate administrative ratios to ensure a high degree of accountability.

In addition to adequate administrative support, reasonable teacher/ student ratios and support personnel ratios (nurses, social workers, counselors, psychologists, secretaries, cooks, and custodians) are fundamental to school system and school effectiveness. Excessive student-teacher ratios and a lack of support personnel can be problematic in meeting the needs of today's students. A reasonable number of students to instruct and a reasonable number of personnel to supervise are characteristics of an effective accountability system.

Programmatic requirements establish program structures that need to be in place in all schools and at the system level. By establishing programmatic requirements in such areas as reading, communication, home-school relations, organization, and standards, efforts to raise academic performance focus on implementation of consistent program opportunities. Defining required programs ensures that students benefit from the same educational opportunities that experts consider to be important for academic success.

PROCESS

Developing Requirements

Minimum requirements need to be determined by professional educators with input from constituent groups. Professional educators with demonstrated teaching and administrative success need to assume the leadership role in establishing organizational requirements.

Much time is consumed by non-educators, particularly board members, discussing the merits of personnel and programmatic organizational requirements. Discussions to determine minimum organizational requirements need to be led by professional educators. Professional educators, with input from constituency groups, students, parents, business, higher education representatives, board members, and community, should determine minimum organizational requirements for schools and school systems.

Educators must take the lead to establish minimum organizational requirements that foster effective schools and school systems. For too long, educators have allowed lack of funding for certain basic organizational requirements to degenerate into endless discussions by "non-experts" on the merits of the basics of quality education. Educators are routinely faced with meeting the needs of all students with inadequate staff, resources, and services. Even the most enthusiastic educator is negatively affected when minimum personnel and programmatic requirements are not provided. Schools and schools systems often achieve good results without the basic organizational requirements. Unfortunately, the personal toll on students, teachers, and administrators results in a high level of personnel burnout, a limited number of schools and school systems functioning at the exemplary level, and fewer students functioning at their maximum potential.

Superintendents should establish committee(s) with representatives from all constituency groups: students, teachers, service personnel, principals, vice principals, curriculum supervisors, administration, board members, higher education business leaders, labor leaders, parents, community members, and senior citizens. Educators who have demonstrated teaching and administrative success should compose the majority of the committee(s). When developing requirements, it is advantageous to include board members to ensure board support and commitment later. It is best to develop the minimum organization requirements during a planning period before a new superintendent takes office. (The practicality of a pre-contract planning/development period for superintendents is discussed under "detractors" to the development process.) At least a three-month planning period is needed to develop minimum requirements. The time is essential to ensure opportunity for input from constituent groups and formal approval by all personnel organizations.

The committee(s) developing requirements should study: (1) needs of their students, school, and community; (2) research on effective schools; and (3) best practice. The committee(s) should generate minimum organizational requirements for their schools and school system and should develop a time frame for input and approval from all personnel organizations prior to submitting organizational requirements to the board. Board members should commit to understanding the requirements and supporting them with funds to establish basic organizational requirements at every level of operation. Establishing organizational requirements focuses all constituents (superintendent, board, community, and personnel) on achieving the essentials of effective school and school system operation and improvement.

Detractors to Developing Requirements

Developing minimum organizational requirements is not necessarily a difficult process, yet it has proven difficult for school systems to accomplish for a number of reasons. First, organizational requirements can and should be used to increase employee accountability. When educators define and implement requirements essential for school and system success, the reasons for lack of student achievement are reduced or eliminated.

Second, organizational requirements necessitate allocation of major funds for implementation. Lack of funding can become the reason for avoiding the process of defining organizational requirements; the process may be thwarted by those who contend that lack of funding for requirements makes it a futile effort. The "nay-sayer" would offer that it is neither reasonable nor common sense to develop personnel and programmatic requirements that are beyond current or immediately projected funding levels. They might dismiss it as "pie in the sky thinking." Unfortunately, without this clear definition of requirements that need to be in place for school and system success, there will always be a lack of comprehensive reform and improvement.

Third, development of organizational requirements necessitates a planning period in which educators work with representatives from various constituent groups to establish agreed-upon personnel and programmatic requirements. A planning period, whether it is before or after a transition to a new administration, is essential to successful development of school and system requirements. Boards may resist providing the necessary planning time, particularly if it involves a pre-superintendent contract period, because of expense and public reaction. It takes considerable time to complete each step in the process: (1) identification of representative teachers, administrators, board, service personnel, community, parents, students, business, industry, and higher education to participate on committees; (2) review of research and best-practice recommendations for personnel and programmatic requirements; (3) development of a consensus on recommended requirements; (4) agreement of teacher, administrator, and service personnel organizations and the board to support recommended requirements; and (5) communication of requirements to employees and constituent groups for input and approval. Like most political entities, boards may find it difficult to commit the time, resources, and support to planning endeavors. However, without sufficient time and involvement, requirements may become the superintendent's mandate rather than a reflection of a consensus by all constituent groups on the essential requirements for school and system success.

Fourth, developing a consensus of the various constituent groups that serve and/or are affected by the school system is difficult. Obtaining consensus can be enhanced when (1) educators who have the expertise to provide necessary research and best-practice to support recommended requirements are selected to lead the development process; (2) boards, administrators, and teachers acknowledge that the purposes for development of requirements outweigh the detractors to the process; and (3) potential committee members agree to achieve consensus on each recommended requirement.

Establishing minimum organizational requirements may be derailed by concerns relating to accountability, funding, planning, and consensus. While each of these concerns needs to be acknowledged, they should not prevent completion of the important task of defining organizational requirements.

SUGGESTED ORGANIZATIONAL REQUIREMENTS

School districts working to establish their own minimum requirements should use the requirements set forth in this chapter as a reference or starting point. The suggested requirements should help administrators, instructors, service and support personnel, board members, higher education instructors, and business and community members focus on defining their own unique personnel and programmatic requirements to ensure equal educational opportunities for all students within their school district. It is important to establish requirements for staffing and programmatic structure. Adequate staffing without well-developed programmatic expectations negatively affects school improvement, as do programmatic expectations without adequate staffing. Programmatic and personnel requirements support each other and both are essential for school and system improvement.

Once requirements are agreed on, it is important that the board makes a public commitment to them. The commitment needs to be long-term, with an understanding that at least a five-year implementation timeline is appropriate. Opportunity for periodic review of personnel and programmatic requirements is necessary to ensure currency with new research and best practice. (Requirements are referenced in Appendix A.) The suggested listing of personnel and programmatic minimum organizational requirements is based upon experience and not necessarily affirmed by research.

MINIMUM ELEMENTARY ORGANIZATIONAL STRUCTURE

Personnel Requirements

Student Enrollment Maximum—500	
Principal	1 per school
Vice principal	1 per 300 students
Counselor	1 per 250 students
Psychologist	1 per 1000 students
Nurse	1 per 750 students
Social worker	1 per 750 students
Teacher	1 to 12 student ratio
Full-day kindergarten	1 teacher/1 aide per 20 students
Primary reading specialist	1 per 250 students
Intermediate reading specialist	1 per 250 students
Art instructor	1 per school
Music instructor	1 per school
Physical education instructor	1 per school
Exceptional student instructor	Per state policy requirements
Secretary	1 per 500 students
Clerk	1 per 300 students
Cook	1 cook per 100 meals—not less than 2 per school
Custodian	1 per 20,000 square feet—not less than 2 per school

Elementary Programmatic Requirements

Communication and Enrichment

- Principal, teacher(s), and support personnel expected to greet students each morning to demonstrate interest in students' wellness and completion of homework assignments and outside reading requirement.

- Afterschool enrichment and assistance program provided to offer a structured opportunity for play, learning, and community involvement.
- Student, principal, and teacher dialogues scheduled to provide opportunities for small groups of students to meet periodically to discuss issues/concerns and make recommendations.
- Art, music, drama, and dance program in which all students participate is provided throughout the school year.

Environment

- School environment clean, comfortable, and attractive.
- All facility code requirements met.

Home/School Relations

- Home visitation program established that expects teachers to make student/home visits.
- Student, parent, and school contracts signed annually—contract outlines parents' responsibility to read to students, assist with homework, support discipline plan, and participate in school activities.
- Parent conferences held a minimum of once each nine weeks. One hour each week is designated as an afterschool conference period, and parents can schedule time to meet with teachers.

Homework

- Fifteen minutes of homework required in primary grades.
- Thirty minutes of homework required in intermediate grades.

Organization

- Uniform student dress enforced that discourages gangs, cliques, and economic labeling.
- Students with special needs included in a regular classes with appropriate support when there is a reasonable expectation that content skills can be mastered.

- Discipline plan implemented that provides for positive reinforcement, defined consequences, and alternative learning center.
- Plan of improvement for the school developed annually.
- Teachers employed on a 210-day contract in order to provide ten extra days for staff development and planning prior to the beginning and at the end of each academic year.
- Teachers' pay routinely increased in order to attract the best and brightest to the field of teaching.

Reading

- Required book reading list developed for each grade.
- Accelerated reading program implemented in all grades.
- Reading Recovery program or comparable program provided *daily* for each first-grade child not meeting minimum reading skill mastery.
- One-to-one remedial reading instruction provided three times per week for each primary-age child not meeting minimum reading skill mastery.
- One-to-one remedial reading instruction provided two times per week for each intermediate age child not meeting minimum reading skill mastery.
- Fifteen minutes of pleasure reading required per day in intermediate grades—parents reading to child or child reading.
- Thirty minutes of pleasure reading required per day in primary grades—parents reading to child or child reading.
- Cassette book assigned to students each week to support pleasure reading.

Standards

- Minimum skill requirements defined for each subject area.
- Students required to write and to speak correctly, clearly, and coherently in each subject area.
- Student proficiency in reading, writing, and math assessed in first through sixth grades.
- An extended time program provided for students who fail to demonstrate proficiency in basic skills.
- Summer programs to support reading/math skill acquisition required of those not mastering minimum skill requirements.

Wellness

- Wellness program for students implemented that provides nutritional food and extensive physical activity.

MINIMUM SECONDARY ORGANIZATIONAL STRUCTURE

Personnel Requirements

Junior High/Middle School Maximum Student—600
High School Maximum Student Enrollment—1200

Principal	1 per school
Vice principal (curriculum, discipline, communication)	1 per 300 students
Counselor	1 per 250 students
Psychologist	1 per 1200 students
Nurse	1 per 750 students
Social worker	1 per 750 students
Teachers	1 per 15 students
Reading specialist	1 per 600 students
Secretary	1 per 500 students
Clerk	1 per 500 students
Cook	1 per 100 meals—not less than 2 per school
Custodian	1 per 20,000 square feet—not less than 2 per school

Secondary Programmatic Requirements

Communication and Enrichment

- Schools required to implement at least one schoolwide project per year with participants from many different disciplines, focusing, for example, on a historical period, a scientific topic, or a musical production.
- Academic advisor assigned to each student.
- Principal and representative teachers required to meet annually with a cross-section of students to discuss concerns and receive recommendations for change.

- Teams or units within schools established to increase student involvement and student/teacher interaction.

Environment

- School environment clean, comfortable, and attractive.
- All facility code requirements met.

Home/School Relations

- Parent conferences held a minimum of once each nine weeks.
- One hour each week is designated as an afterschool conference period when parents can schedule time to meet with teachers.

Homework

- Forty-five minutes of homework in grades seven through nine required each day.
- Sixty to ninety minutes of homework required in grades nine through twelve each day.

Organization

- Career clusters for specific courses of study provided in at least the following or similar areas (high schools offer the basic courses for each cluster): health, human services, engineering and technology, science and natural resources, business and marketing, fine arts, and humanities.
- Career major declared by each student at the end of tenth grade. Students have the flexibility to move or change their intent.
- Tracking students by ability and lower-level classes eliminated; students provided with a challenging course of study.
- Students with special needs included in regular classes with appropriate support when there is a reasonable expectation that content skills can be mastered.
- Schools offer a variety of advanced placement courses with high standards for enrollment; students encouraged to participate.
- Driver's education offered after school hours and during the summer.

- By the end of the eighth grade, all students required to develop a general plan of study that identifies the student's core curriculum, career cluster, and educational path for grades nine and ten. All courses selected meet the requirements of the student's educational plan, which is revised annually.
- Student assistance team required to intervene with students at risk.
- Discipline plan implemented that provides positive reinforcement and specific consequences for inappropriate behavior.
- Alternative education schools provided for students who need to continue their education outside of the regular school setting.
- Uniform student dress code exists and is monitored to discourage gangs, cliques, and economic labeling.
- One technology lab provided for every 300 students enrolled.
- Structured tutoring opportunities provided for students in all subject areas.
- School plan of improvement developed on an annual basis.
- Teachers employed on a 210-day contract in order to provide extra ten days for staff development and planning prior to the beginning and at the end of each academic year.
- Teacher pay routinely increased in order to attract the best and brightest to the field of teaching.

Reading

- Designated book reading list required for each grade.
- Accelerated reading program or similar incentive program implemented in all grades.
- Remedial reading instruction program provided for all students with significant reading skill deficiencies.

Standards

- Curriculum structure divided into three parts: rigorous *core* required of all students; elective group to support the student's *educational path*; elective group to support the student's *career cluster*.
- Standard course requirements that reflect high expectations is identified and monitored in all courses in grades seven through twelve. The requirements include reading lists, oral presentations, laboratory experiences, written compositions, technology applications, and projects.

- Students required to meet the following minimum core curriculum requirements: English: 4.0 credits; mathematics: 4.0 credits (At least two of the four math credits are Algebra I or Applied Math II and a higher mathematics course); science: 3.0 credits; social studies: 4.0 credits; fine arts: 1.0 credit; fitness and wellness: 1.0 credit; computer application: 1.0 credit; careers and life skills seminar: 0.5–1.0 credit; speech 0.5–1.0 credit.
- At least one course in the fine or performing arts required for all students. This course will not be an alternative to foreign language or applied arts.
- Career seminar course required. Seminar includes in-depth career exploration, consumer and economic skills, and personal and life skills, and emphasizes community service and the work ethic. Specific requirements include declaring a career major and extending the education plan to include grades eleven and twelve and post-secondary goals.
- Community service learning requirement expected to be met by all students.
- A focused program of study preparing students for postsecondary study in either university or technical training provided. All students complete high standard core requirements regardless of pathway:

    College Preparatory: Core curriculum and courses required for entrance into two- or four-year college, including two units of foreign language

    Technical Preparation: Core curriculum.

    Associate Degree: Required college preparatory program leading to a two-year associate degree; and program of studies focusing on a particular technical area.

    Technical Certificate: Core curriculum; completion of vocational program in the home school or a vocational center; and graduating seniors required to successfully complete an individual graduation study project.
- Correct grammar and speech required to be used by students in all classes.
- Proficiency in reading, writing and math assessed in sixth, seventh, and eighth grades.
- Extended time program provided for students who fail to demonstrate basic skill proficiency.
- Dual credit courses, advanced placement courses, honors, summer programs, and testing out of required course provided in high school program.

- Students in college preparatory or associate degree pathway required to take either the SAT or ACT tests by the end of their junior year.

Wellness

- An intensive health course required in grades seven and eight with strong components dealing with nutrition; the effects of nicotine, drugs, and alcohol; and human sexuality, including teenage pregnancy and sexually transmitted diseases.
- Wellness programs for students in place that support nutritional food and extensive physical activity.

MINIMUM ORGANIZATION REQUIREMENTS FOR A SCHOOL SYSTEM

Personnel Requirements

Superintendent	
Deputy Superintendent	
Treasurer	
Associate or Assistant Superintendent	School administration, direct monitoring responsibility for schools. Staffed at a ratio of one to ten schools, not to exceed 5000 students.
	Business
	Finance
	Personnel
	Communications
	Instruction
Director/Coordinator/	
Supervisory-Level Positions	Federal programs
	Exceptional children
	Technology
	Accounting
	Information systems
	Research
	Alternative programs
	Vocational education
	Support services—Health, social work

Transportation

Food service
Personnel
Communication
Curriculum/instruction
Maintenance
Facilities

Minimum Ratio of Central Office
Administrators to Teachers

Utilize current mean ratio of number of
central office administrators to teachers
based upon current Education Research
Service Ratios

CENTRAL OFFICE ADMINISTRATIVE PROGRAMMATIC REQUIREMENTS

Management and Organization

- Management system improvement process and minimum organizational requirements defined and formally approved by the board.
- Management plan implemented that defines management organizational structure, principles and priorities, and method of operation.
- Management plan approved by the board.
- System of management, as defined in the plan, required to involve more people in the decision-making process and is

TABLE 1.1   1997–98 Data Enrollment Group

Number of students	Mean number of teachers per central office administrator
25,000+	45.1
10,000–24,999	39.0
2,500–9,999	32.6
300–2,499	29.1
Total all groups	35.4

Source: Education Research Service 1998

driven by what is right for children, not by compromise and politics.

- Management team established that includes superintendent, deputy superintendent, and all associate and assistant superintendents and representatives from elementary, secondary principal association, and teacher organization.
- Management team directly responsible for development and implementation of the annual system objective and work objective plan to achieve the board's vision.
- Management team required to check that system objectives addressed at all levels of operation.
- Management team required to serve as a role model for team-building at all levels within the school.
- Management team required to provide to board members reliable, timely information regarding the school system's operation.
- Standards for performance defined at all levels of operation.
- Monitoring system established that ensures a high level of accountability at every operational level.
- Process established for intervening in schools not making sufficient progress in meeting standards.
- Communication model plan established to monitor vehicles that provide and receive information from and to each constituent group.
- Area assistant superintendents directly accountable for a specific number of schools and completion of the following:
  - Working with the schools to achieve the board's vision and the system objectives;
  - Identifying the school's financial, physical, and human resource needs;
  - Coordinating area support teams to provide improved delivery of services to students and school staff members;
  - Identifying and coordinating school system and community resources for area schools;
  - Assisting and monitoring each in the development, implementation and assessment of individual school improvement plans;
  - Developing a network for increased parent-community awareness, involvement, and support of quality education at the local level; and
  - Monitoring and assessing the performance of each school principal.

Improvement Process

- System objectives approved by the board.
- The process for developing system objectives required to include:
  - Opportunity for input at all levels and from all constituent groups of the school system;
  - Analyzing data;
  - Defining succinct, measurable objectives;
  - Outlining supportive activities;
  - Communicating determined objectives to all constituent groups;
  - Implementing and monitoring objective completion; and
  - Evaluating completion of objectives and success in bringing about improvement.
- System objectives identified annually for at least the following areas:
  - Instruction;
  - Fiscal responsibility;
  - Communication;
  - Operations; and
  - Facilities.
- Annual report required to summarize progress made in accomplishing each system objective.
- Management team members' evaluations based upon completion and or progress in accomplishing each system objective.

SUMMARY

Development of minimum organizational requirements is an essential component for school and system success. Establishment and successful implementation of personnel and programmatic requirements affects all facets of school system operation and improvement. Requirements enhance school systems' ability to "keep the train on the track, lay new track, and keep peace in the valley."

Minimum requirements focus all constituent groups on achievement of a common purpose. Educators need to assume a leadership role in development of minimum personnel and programmatic requirements that need to be in place if all students are to receive a quality education within their school district. Educators have often been reluctant to establish essential requirements for staff, programs, and services for operating successful schools. This reluctance needs to be replaced with educators, who have garnered expertise through education and experience, and who understand and can determine personnel and programmatic requirements essential for students, schools, and system success. Educators must also provide the leadership to advocate for sufficient funds to support implementation of all requirements. Educators need to articulate that boards and communities have a responsibility to appropriate funds that establish a basic structure that ensures quality of educational opportunities for all students. Boards should take formal action to approve recommendations and serve as leaders to support and seek adequate funding for staff and programmatic requirements.

Appropriate communication vehicles need to be in place to ensure that all constituent groups provide input into the development of requirements and receive sufficient information on the recommended requirements. Educational programs, brochures, conferences, television, radio, newspaper articles, and media advertisements need to be used to communicate to employees and the community the requirements essential for students, schools, and system success. All constituent groups need to understand that if essential personnel and programmatic structure are not in place, then outcomes at all levels may be negatively affected. The concept that public educators can educate all children to acquire the same competencies within thirteen years without adequate staff, programs, services, and facilities needs to be changed.

Organizational requirements enhance the accountability of employees, boards, and the community. Employees must assume more responsibility for student performance if defined requirements for success are in place. Boards must assume a leadership role in communicating, supporting, and advocating for minimum requirements, while communities must assume responsibility for funding minimum requirements.

Establishment of minimum organizational requirements is one of three components that needs to be developed by boards, administration, teachers, service personnel, and constituent groups if school systems are to be successful. The second component for making school systems work is the establishment of a management system featuring a high level of accountability for students and employees. Chapter 2 establishes a rationale and describes an effective management system.

CHAPTER 2

Management System

Destiny is not a matter of change; it is a matter of choice; it is not
a thing to be waited for, it is a thing to be achieved.

—WILLIAM JENNINGS BRYAN, QUOTED IN JIM NEFF, *MEA INSIDER*

Begin with the end in mind.

—STEVEN COVEY, *FIRST THINGS FIRST*

INTRODUCTION

A management system that features accountability at every level of operation needs to be developed, understood, and supported. "Keeping a
school system on the track" and at the same time "laying new track" for
improvement initiatives and "keeping peace in the valley" requires a
well-defined management system. It is the superintendent's job to clearly
define and articulate the components of the management system. To be
effective, management systems have formal support of board members
defined within the superintendent's contract or through board policy.

This chapter provides the rationale and support for management systems that generate a high level of accountability and describes the various components of an effective management system that are replicable in
other school districts.

In order to understand the importance of an effective management
system, superintendents and boards should be given a rationale for
establishing a management system that provides for a high level of
accountability. It has become politically expedient to bash administrators
and administrative structures. Justification to support a management system that provides for a sufficient number of administrators to effectively
manage the school system is important information for superintendents

27

and boards to have readily accessible and to understand. The first section of this chapter reviews the literature on management systems and provides rationale for establishment of an effective management system for school system operation and improvement.

The second section of this chapter reviews the components of an effective management system that is based on enhancing accountability at every level, and at the same time supporting site-based decision-making and school/system improvement. Implementation of an effective management system should result in a significant level of improvement in instruction, communication, finance, operations, and facilities.

RATIONALE AND SUPPORT FOR MANAGEMENT SYSTEM STRUCTURE

A central tenant of organizational thought is that administration is essential to improving any organization. Henri Fayol, a modern organization theorist, defined administration in terms of five functions: planning, organizing, commanding, leading or coordinating, and evaluating results or controlling (Owens 1991, 5). These functions need to be incorporated into the daily operation of a school district's management system. They must be included in annual local school and county improvement plans and be the basis for development, modification, and implementation of policy and the development of effective decision-making processes.

Administrative functions of planning organizing, commanding, coordinating, and evaluating remain inherent and necessary in all types of effective administrative organizations. Although the term *bureaucracy* has in recent years received its share of negative publicity, it is a far advancement from authoritarian managers and political patronage systems of the past.

Central to classical organization theory of management is the concept of hierarchy, meaning the line and staff relationships. The general rule that responsibility and authority should flow in a direct and unbroken path is central to the hierarchical concept that one receives orders only from one individual. Max Weber compared hierarchical administration as the "routinizing" of administration to that of a machine "routinizing" production. Weber, who is credited with the first comprehensive definition of bureaucracy, included hierarchical supervision as a major characteristic of administrative structures (Morgan 1986, 25). As organizations and work have become more complex, the hierarchical alignment has been greatly modified to support some functional administration, such as having specialists in given areas provide the necessary leadership and orders. The complexity of school systems makes a single chain of command insufficient (Morgan 1989, 44).

Until recently, school organization charts typically reflected a vertical or hierarchical relationship. Given the complexities and size of many school districts, the advancement of organizational structures that allow for decision-making at the lowest level have gained wide acceptance. School employees need opportunity to better understand their job responsibilities and to have more control over their work achievements, successes, and failures. "Everyone in schools must believe in the power . . . and the ability to change our performance and our environment" (Fields 1993, 82). Organizational theory supports limiting the span of control (employees per supervisor) in order to increase productivity and accountability. The importance of this limiting span grows as site-based decision-making practices have increased. General principles of classical management theory define "span of control" as being not so large that it creates problem of coordination and communication (Morgan 1986, 26). Many scholars as well as administrators believe that hierarchical or scalar organizational principals with a limited span of control, structured accountability programs, competency-based instructional programs, and management by objectives are essential components for administrative practice today (Owens 1991, 8).

A management system based on effective hierarchical organizational arrangement with functional control must be accompanied by a management philosophy that ensures constant attention to an improvement or quality process. The management philosophy should support a quality improvement process that encourages everyone in the organization to define and to continuously pursue quality, all day every day, and with every act and decision support the organization's achievement of purpose (Kaufman and Zahn 1983, 11). In addition, through its administrative team, the management system must be committed to establishing standards and defining accountability. "Until the basic school learning processes have some semblance of performance quality, reliability and cost quality, schools will continue to flounder without a base from which to operate" (Fields 1994, 61). School systems should establish for each subject area: (1) core competency requirements; (2) minimum performance standards for students and employees; and (3) specific accountability procedures to evaluate and report progress in defined areas.

The standards and accountability procedures must be part of a defined system objective development process. Many states have defined core competencies for specific subject areas. An example of West Virginia's objectives for Algebra I is illustrated in Table 2.1. The addition of minimum requirements in reading, writing, speaking, career exploration, and project development for each subject area further establishes a standard of performance and expectation for teacher instruction. Table 2.2 provides an example of Kanawha County School's established performance requirements for the

TABLE 2.1

West Virginia State Goals and Objectives
Kanawha County Schools Mathematics
NCTM Strands emphasized, adopted text location, other supplementary sources,
and reinforced by KCS minimum course requirements

NCTM STRANDS
1. Problem Solving 4. Connections 7. Geometry from Synthetic Perspective 10. Statistics 13. Calculus
2. Communication 5. Algebra 8. Geometry from a Algebraic Perspective 11. Probability 14. Mathematical Structure

OBJECTIVES (+workplace; *tested)

Algebra I	NCTM STRANDS														Test Location	Other Sources	Minimum Requirements
	1	2	3	4	5	6	7	8	9	10	11	12	13	14			
A1.1 (9,10,11) simplify numerical and evaluate algebraic expressions using grouping symbols and order of operations (*)	x	x	x	x	x	x	x	x							pp 13–17		See technology lessons; Reading-historical Connection in each chapter (see index); Speaking
A1.2 (9,10,11) translate word phrases into algebraic expressions and word sentences into equations or inequalities (+;*)	x	x	x	x	x	x	x	x							pp 36–39 pp 176–180		Speaking
A1.3 justify steps in the simplification	x	x	x	x	x	x	x	x							pp 31–35		Speaking
A1.4 (9,10,11) solve multi-step linear equations and inequalities in one variable and apply the skills toward solving practical problems (+;*)	x	x	x	x	x				x						pp 111–115 pp 186–190		Speaking Experiments; Projects (1)
A1.5 (9,10,11) solve literal equations (i.e. formulas) for a given variable and apply the skills toward solving practical problems and better equip students for calculator usage (+;*)	x	x	x	x	x	x	x	x		x					pp 122–125 practical app. Chap. 4, pp.132–173		Speaking; Career; Experiments Projects (1)
A1.6 (9,10,11) analyze a given set of data for the existence of a pattern represent the pattern algebraically and graphically, determine the domain and range, and determine if the relation is a function (+;*)	x	x	x	x	x	x	x	x		x	x	x		x	Chap. 9, pp 352–396		Speaking
A1.7 solve absolute value equations in one variable and interpret the results on a number line (+;*)	x	x	x	x	x		x	x		x					pp 199–203		Speaking

major subject areas of English, social studies, math, and science at the tenth-grade level. Both the subject area objectives and the minimum requirements illustrate standards that school districts need to have in place to measure student and teacher performance, core competencies, and minimum requirements. Measures of performance should always be applied against a standard. Effective management systems require and support the establishment of core competencies and minimum requirements in order to achieve a high level of accountability.

The management system must, through its administration, work collaboratively with its board to define goals and then annually develop objectives and activities to accomplish the goals. The process of annually developing system objectives and work objectives involves all participants: employees, superintendent, board, students, parents, and community. Coupled with the development of system objectives, a strong evaluation model that determines the degree of success in each objective is necessary (Carver 1990, 63).

An effective management system requires statistical tools to determine need and gather data that assess progress. Once need is established and degree of progress is ascertained, this information is utilized to make decisions and set direction (Kaufman and Zahn 1983, 41). This philosophical commitment to statistical and factual information analysis is an important part of a management system. Management team members must utilize comprehensive needs assessment procedures prior to establishing system and school objectives. Assessment of need results in defined areas for the development of objectives (Kaufman and Zahn, 1983, 74).

Finally, the management system must establish in personnel a willingness to work as part of an empowered team in which members are valued for their own worth, work together in a caring and cooperative manner, and are held accountable for their performance (Kaufman and Zahn 1983, 10). This method of operation—involvement plus accountability—is incorporated into a comprehensive communication philosophy that ensures students, employees, community, and board members understand how the management system operates. This involvement and accountability philosophy of an effective management/organization structure is defined by Zahn in his Management Model and illustrated in Table 2.3 (Kaufman and Zahn 1983, 11).

Zahn's three-pyramid management model is based on a total quality management approach (TQM). The model defines three areas that must be incorporated in a management model for progress to occur. First, a defined systemic quality improvement process is part of everyone's daily

TABLE 2.2

Kanawha County Schools
Minimum Requirements
Grade 10

	English	Social Studies	Geometry	Science
Reading: 6 Books Articles Documents	Directed (2) Independent (2), may be with content areas. In addition: selected short stories, poetry, non-fiction	Three primary sources	2 readings per course–course-related (suggested Internet usage)	9 "current topic" articles
Writing	Informal (daily opportunities); Formal (5 opportunities using writing process) must include research; Creative Expression (1) Time writing with prompt emphasis: Multiparagraph composition with thesis, sentence variety and transitions, structured revision, editing	3-5 page report distinguishing primary and secondary sources	Continue Portfolio development; Maintain a vocabulary section in notebook to include definition, sketches; Incorporate multiple methods of proof (paragraph, flow chart 2 column, etc.); 2 investigative reports per unit from Geometer's sketch pad	9 critiques (one of which could be on career); 2 research report with primary and secondary sources using MLA style and including Internet sources; 1 summation (results and conclusion); 2 formal lab reports; 1 statement of limitations for a specific experiment
Speaking Formal Informal	Formal (1); Informal (multiple opportunities); Creative	1 presentation; 1 as a reporter for a cooperative group	1 presentation related to project (whole class/group); 1 as a reporter for a cooperative group	4 presentations (1 of which could be on a career) individually or in teams: –contrast the three ways of reporting data variation –defend a "line of best fit" on a graph
Career	1. Prepare career research paper; 2. Resume Emphasis: Teamwork through cooperative learning experiences	To emphasize teamwork, 10% of the time students will engage in cooperative learning	To emphasize teamwork 10% of the time students will engage in cooperative learning	See writing/speaking
Experiments/Projects	Research project	Service learning project	Use scientific calculation, MIRAS, geoboards, compass and or other appropriate material; 2 projects: –1 focusing on careers in math –1 focusing on geometry in the world utilize Internet resources)	Actively seek solutions to the explorations and experiments in each unit. At least 50% of the constructivist learning cycle requires hands-on, minds-on activities which shall include: 8 wet labs; 10 computer-based labs using 10 different electronic probes as part of thematic modules

All Grade Levels

Writes legibly
Uses a variety of graphic organizers
Demonstrates understanding of writing process
Shows proficiency with word processor
One independent reading (8–12) will be summer reading

operation, and everyone understands and is committed to their own ability and desire to make a difference in system improvement. Second, decisions are based on statistical information that is generated from an analysis of student performance professional staff, and programs. Third, everything that is accomplished is a reflection of individuals who understand their own responsibility and authority within the organization, and who are able to work together in a forthright, caring manner (Kaufman and Zahn 1983, 11). In conclusion, an effective management system is important for the daily operation of a school system as well as for system improvement. An effective management system includes: (1) hierarchical structure with functional administrative authority closest to the students; (2) limited span of control; and (3) defined quality management philosophy that supports continuous improvement in all areas of operation. The

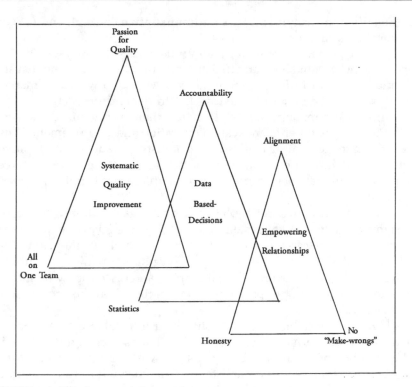

FIGURE 2.1 (Kaufman and Zahn, 11)

management system described in the next section incorporates these characteristics.

COMPONENTS OF AN EFFECTIVE MANAGEMENT SYSTEM: AN OVERVIEW

An effective management system must achieve two purposes: (1) address the tasks, concerns, and issues necessary for the daily operation of the system; and (2) bring about comprehensive system improvement. This section describes the components of a management system that provides for a high level of accountability at every operational level through reasonable supervisory ratios and site-based decision-making. These management system components include: (1) structure of a management team; (2) principles and priorities that require an improvement and evaluation structure; (3) area administrative concept; and (4) communication strategies.

An effective management system must support the system's vision and mission. Establishing an efficient and effective management system should be a priority for superintendents. Without a workable management system, the superintendent is left to depend on each individual administrator's management style rather than an organized, collective effort to provide for efficient system operation and improvement. With a defined management system, each administrator and most employees understand how problems are addressed, policies are enforced, improvement strategies are planned and implemented, and performance is monitored.

A superintendent's initial plans and activities should revolve around designing a management system that supports the level of planning and accountability necessary to move forward, and at the same time addresses all daily operational needs. Consultation with representatives of higher education, review of the literature, and discussion with individuals and constituent groups connected with the school system are necessary steps.

Involvement of higher education is instrumental in the development of a management system that is supported by research and best practice. The superintendent needs to establish a working relationship with a higher education institution and then conference with professors in the department of education administration and request assistance in the development of an effective management system for the school district. A management system must be supported by individuals with expertise in education administration research in order to effectively address potential criticism or concern related to a proposed management structure. A request for advice and counsel from those in higher education fosters a willingness in professors to become involved in the successful implementation of a management system. Professors may agree to serve as mentors and advisors to the school system's administrative team. Establishing vehicles for obtaining on-going advice from higher education professors is important.

MANAGEMENT TEAM

An effective management system requires the formation of a management team consisting of an associate team, an assistant team, and representatives from the elementary and secondary principal and teacher association.

The associate team should include the superintendent and such positions as deputy superintendent, treasurer, business manager, legal counsel, associate superintendents, and director of communications. (To enhance communication effort, the director of communications should participate in all meetings.) The associate team should have the primary responsibility of management of legal services, finance, business, curriculum, communication, operation, and administration for the school system.

The assistant team should be chaired by the deputy superintendent and consist of all assistant superintendents (curriculum, staff development, communication, and so on) and area assistant superintendents. The assistant team's primary focus should be school improvement. The assistant team should also review and approve all administrative recommendations that affect school operation. The assistant team has the primary and direct responsibility of supervising schools. The deputy superintendent should define the agendas for the assistant meetings and ensure communication with the associate level team. Assistant team members are responsible for communicating information to staff who report directly to them. Area assistant superintendents for schools should conduct regular meetings with area principals and assigned support personnel, such as psychologists, specialists, itinerant teachers, and social workers. Principals should communicate with staff and constituency: students, parents, and community members (local school improvement councils). The management, associate, assistant, area, school, and department meeting process establishes a communication network that disseminates and collects information. This process offers an opportunity to receive direct input from all constituents when developing annual objectives and determining a system's progress, needs, concerns, tasks, and issues.

The management team should have representatives from elementary and secondary principal and teacher associations. Problems in communication and support are lessened when a teacher representative serves on the management team. The cost and time away from the classroom for the teacher representatives may be a concern. However, this concern can be addressed by identifying a long-term substitute for the teacher(s) representatives to ensure consistency of instruction. The entire management team, consisting of associate and assistant teams and representatives from both elementary and secondary principal and teacher associations, should meet at least once a month with the superintendent. The primary focus of the management team is to establish annual system (focus and work) objectives, monitor their completion, and address major operational issues and responsibilities.

Just as individuals need principles to guide their behavior, so does a management system that is dependent on individuals for its implementation. The principles and priorities recommended for an effective management system are based on school reform efforts in Kentucky. There, the principles and priorities defined for management system operation support the board's vision and purpose. The following are recommended principles defined for an effective management team/system operation.

MANAGEMENT TEAM PRINCIPLES

1. The management team defines the system objectives and priorities to achieve the board's vision.
2. The management team develops and implements a monitoring system that manages all aspects of operation within the school system.
3. The management team serves as a role model for team-building at all levels within the school system.
4. The management team designs a system of management that is democratic, that involves more people in the decision-making process, and that is driven by beliefs (what is right for children) than by compromise and politics.
5. The management team ensures that beliefs and actions (system objectives) are incorporated in all levels of operation.
6. The management team provides reliable, timely information regarding the operation of the school system to all board members (Kentucky Reform Act).

The first principle requires the management team to annually develop system (focus) objectives and subsequent work objectives or activities. This annual definition of system objectives is critical to the entire improvement process effort. Determining system objectives and activities is the most time-consuming responsibility for the management team. Developing and implementing the activities to accomplish the objectives is a year-long endeavor. (The system objective process is detailed in Chapter 3.) The system objective process includes: (1) arranging opportunity for input at all levels and from all constituent groups of the school system; (2) analyzing data; (3) defining succinct, measurable objectives; (4) outlining supportive activities; (5) communicating determined objectives to all constituent groups; (6) implementing and monitoring objective completion; and (7) evaluating degree of objective completion and success in bringing about improvement.

The developing, implementing, and monitoring of system objectives is an ongoing process that requires the management team to focus on moving the system forward as it addresses the mountain of daily crises, tasks, and issues. The objective-driven method of management should be incorporated into the personnel evaluation process at all levels. The superintendent's evaluation should be based on each defined system objective and the determined level of achievement. Evaluation of top-level management positions should be based on the defined system objectives (see Appendix B for an example of a Superintendent's Evaluation Instrument based on system objectives). Employees should be evaluated in light of specific system objectives and supportive activities.

A second principle of the management team is to develop, implement, and monitor a system that effectively manages and supports all aspects of school system operation. The system objective process satisfies this principle because individuals at each level of operation are expected to develop work objectives that support system objectives. An annual report on system accomplishments should formally document progress in each school, department, and attendance area. Monitoring of students, employees, schools, departments, offices, and school system progress is an important part of an effective management system. A level of accountability must be established for students, teachers, and administrators in the school system. Personnel evaluations should address defined levels of accountability and relate to system objectives. School, office, department, and project objectives and activities should support the system objectives. Annual review of evaluation reports from schools, departments, and projects should be incorporated into a comprehensive annual progress report. State accreditation standards should be used to provide necessary data for developing system objectives and monitoring school and system progress. Correlation of system objectives with state accreditation standards is important for eliminating duplication of work, increasing accountability, and enhancing objective monitoring and evaluation of all aspects of system operation.

There must be a process for intervening in schools not making sufficient progress in meeting accreditation standards or school objectives. Schools need to meet the minimum requirements in student performance on standardized test measures. Standards must be set for other measures of school effectiveness, including graduation rate, dropout rate, attendance, grades, parental involvement, and customer satisfaction. An area assistant superintendent must focus on schools that do not meet the minimum defined standards in any area and help define objectives and activities to bring about progress.

Schools must be expected to show progress in annual school reports. An intervention process should be initiated in schools that show no or little improvement. The intervention process entails five basic steps:

- *Step 1:* The process begins with a comprehensive review of school data by an area assistant superintendent, an associate superintendent of curriculum, a team of support personnel, and the building principal. The review process affords each principal the opportunity to communicate problems and concerns at the school level that affect school progress. General areas of need should be identified.
- *Step 2:* The principal, area assistant superintendent, and associate superintendent identify personnel who might help recommend strategies to bring about school progress. The support personnel should constitute a school improvement support team. This team's composition varies based on individual school needs, but generally, it should include teachers and principals from other schools, support personnel (curriculum, health, social special education, and reading specialists), building principal, faculty senate president, and a higher education faculty member.
- *Step 3:* School improvement support team reviews student and employee data and schedules visits to school for initial observations. The observations or visits include observations of all classrooms and review of lesson plans and instructional strategies utilized. Observations should include analysis of classroom management, teaching techniques, presence of defined high standards of performance, and accountability processes. Visits should also include meetings with representative groups of students, teachers, service personnel, and parents to discuss needs, concerns, and recommendations. A follow-up report should summarize strength and weaknesses identified through observation and meetings.
- *Step 4:* School improvement support team develops a plan of action for school improvement. The plan clearly defines needs that have been determined by a review of data, observation, and conferences; existing or proposed school objectives that should be addressed; activities recommended for achieving objectives; any additional cost that the school cannot meet; timeline for implementing all activities; and an evaluation model.
- *Step 5:* School improvement support team monitors implementation of the improvement plan. The improvement support team may need on-site staff assistance to implement work activities. In all instances, a regular schedule for members of the on-site team to visit and monitor progress is developed and followed. The support team is required to issue a mid-timeline and end of timeline report.

The third and fourth principles acknowledge the importance of site-based decision-making and a democratic style of leadership. The principles further reinforce the need for a high level of involvement of those affected by the decision. The principles support Deming's theories of business management, which holds that when managers treat workers as partners rather than underlings, productivity will increase (Kaufman and Zahn 1983, 10). Working teams with common purpose are an instrumental part of an effective management system because they embody the literature's conclusions about involving people on teams:

1. Improves degree of implementation;
2. Enhances learning of all team members;
3. Improves information and action levels;
4. Increases opportunity to correct errors earlier on; and
5. Increases risk-taking. (Oswald 1996)

Examples of site-based decision strategies that should be implemented in an effective management system include the formation of the management team; the division of the school system into attendance areas; the establishment of meetings with all representative groups, principals, teachers, service personnel, and students; the definition of a process for problem-solving; the establishment of a school improvement process; and the increased and realignment of funds to the school level. The management team concept supports team-building of faculty senates and local school improvement councils. Requests for policy waivers, new policy approval, and new program initiatives must also demonstrate that opportunity for input from faculty senates and local school improvement councils was received. Effective management systems support individual opinion, local decision-making, team-building, and involvement of constituent groups in system improvement.

The fifth principle of an effective management team/system emphasizes a commitment of effort to system objectives at every level of operation. If only the associate level team is knowledgeable and committed to system objectives, the chance of progress is greatly diminished. An effective management system is based on involvement and teamwork and requires that everyone understand the focus objectives. To ensure this broad commitment, all school, office, and department annual improvement plans should be reviewed by a member of the management team for consistency with system objectives. New projects or initiatives must demonstrate support for system objective(s). Personnel evaluation measures and annual evaluation reports should reflect progress in meeting system objective(s).

The sixth principle of an effective management team/system recognizes the importance of making the board part of the team initiative to bring about school and system improvement. System objectives must relate to the board's vision and priorities. System objectives should be reviewed and discussed with the board at the beginning of the school year. The board should be given an annual written report of progress, along with quarterly updates. Extensive communication efforts should be established to ensure board involvement. The superintendent should develop a weekly activity report to provide information to the board about activities designed to accomplish board's vision and system objectives. The activity report should also inform the board about major issues and crises that occurred during the week.

Once principles are defined for the management system, the system's priorities need to be established. Priorities guide the development of system objectives, serve as a basis for making decisions regarding regulations and policy, and provide support for specific personnel, program, and service changes or initiatives. Priorities should support the establishment of a management-level team and subsequent teams at all level of operation that are knowledgeable, well informed, and committed to implementing the best educational practices in the most efficient, cost-effective, and caring environment. The following examples of priorities should be considered in an effective management system.

MANAGEMENT TEAM PRIORITIES

1. Rebuild the administrative structure into a decentralized, customer-driven service organization that involves and responds to the needs of key constituencies: students, parents, employees, and community organizations.

2. Acknowledge that centralization in management is appropriate only where necessary to achieve economies of scale (purchasing, food service, and so on) and/or to take advantage of expertise that may not be available at the local level (staff development and personnel/legal counsel).

3. Support objectives, policies, regulations, and procedures that allow for efficient interaction, minimize paperwork, reduce delays, and increase responsibility and accountability.

4. Adopt a management style centered on support and continuing communication with schools through daily interaction and presence in the schools.

5. Empower those at all levels to make decisions and take responsibility for their actions.

6. Recognize that the most important work of education takes place at the school and classroom level, and that effective leadership provides necessary support and assistance to bring about improvement.
7. Pursue fiscal responsibility by increasing efficiency and instituting cost-cutting practices.
8. Provide and encourage staff development that improves personnel performance at all levels (Kentucky Reform Act).

The established priorities should support the principles and the board's vision. In order to be consistently utilized in daily activities and duties, priorities need to be understood by the board and the management team. Communicate priorities and principles to all employees and constituent groups through a variety of communication vehicles: meetings, articles, brochures, and television.

AREA CONCEPT

An effective management system supports site-based decision-making. Effective management systems limit the span of control. Central office management personnel need to be accessible to schools if site-based decision-making is encouraged and supported. Management systems need to organize administrative structures so that there is a reasonable number of schools in each supervisory unit. (For example, an assistant superintendent of schools should supervise no more than fifteen schools with a total enrollment that does not exceed 7,500 students.) Effective management systems should reflect a decentralized administration. Large school systems require division into more manageable organizational structures. Elementary, junior high, and middle schools that feed into a given high school should be clustered together within a geographical area of supervision. These clusters of schools should constitute an administrative area that is supervised by an assistant superintendent. Each geographical administrative area should have support staff, including special education specialists, social workers, nurses, psychologists, itinerant teachers, and homebound teachers. Area assistant superintendents and support teams should be relocated to local school buildings. Locating assistant superintendents and support, personnel within school buildings enhances daily accountability, support, and level of service. An effective management system includes defined responsibilities for area assistant superintendents that support the established principles and priorities and correlate with system objectives. The following are examples of defined responsibilities for area assistant superintendents:

1.   Work directly with schools achieve the board's vision and management team's priorities, principles, and the system objectives;
2.   Identify schools' financial, physical, and human resource needs;
3.   Coordinate area support teams to improve delivery of services to students and school staff members;
4.   Identify and coordinate school system and community resources for area schools;
5.   Assist schools with the development, implementation, and assessment of individual school improvement plans;
6.   Develop a network for increased parent-community awareness, involvement, and support of quality education at the local level;
7.   Monitor and assess the performance of school principals; and
8.   Provide continuous opportunities for staff development.

The establishment of area management units for supervision is critical to system accountability. In school systems that manage many schools, the ability to support and assess school progress can be negatively affected by an administrative structure that affords limited supervision and involvement. Frequent contact and involvement by the central office administration at the local level is essential for establishing responsibility and accountability.

The area concept of administration is an important component of an effective management system. The area concept supports local empowerment, increases support, limits span of control, and increases accountability at every level of operation. Through the establishment of administrative areas of supervision, problems, concerns, issues, and crises are addressed in a much more expedient and involved manner. An area assistant superintendent located at the school building level should not be considered as an administrator making a decision in a remote location but as an individual who is part of school community. With increased involvement and participation in individual assigned schools, area assistant superintendents and support personnel become more directly involved in the school improvement process and in personnel accountability. "Not knowing" becomes an infrequent excuse for failure to implement a directive, a policy, or program improvement when assistant superintendents are assigned to a given group of schools and are physically located in a school.

COMMUNICATION STRATEGIES OF AN
EFFECTIVE MANAGEMENT SYSTEM

Clearly defined communication strategies are essential for all aspects of school system operation and are characteristic of an effective management system. The ability to effectively communicate the intent, purpose, or outcome of a given situation, plan, or decision directly relates to the level of acceptance of those affected.

The superintendent is the key communicator for the school system. He or she serves as a good listener and conveys what is heard into appropriate action. The effectiveness of any management system is often contingent on everyone's understanding of role and responsibilities. Sending a clear message that the superintendent is interested in people's opinion is critical. Superintendents must act to institute change based on the school system's defined needs. The superintendent must clearly communicate actions taken so the message is not only received but understood. Superintendents must be aware of communication gaps in the system and should develop structures to ascertain the level of understanding of various messages communicated (Patterson 1997, 15).

Figure 2.2 is a model communication synergy cycle that should be used to determine if there is a continuous effort to keep all constituents informed and involved at every level of operation. The synergy cycle identifies the vehicles utilized for information to flow to and from each constituent group: students, school personnel, department/office staff, management team, board, and community. "Leaders have a responsibility to check regularly to make sure the organization truly understands what is intended to be communicated . . . the communication needs to occur in multiple ways, including one-to-one, town meeting formats, written updates by the leaders of the change initiative, as well as books and articles" (Patterson 1998, n.p.).

For some constituent groups, appropriate vehicles are not in place for good communication. If gaps exist, then appropriate vehicles (services or programs) need to be established. For example, all school districts hold regularly scheduled structured meetings that provide opportunities for boards, the superintendent, management team, the community, and employees to communicate and express concerns. Such opportunities include regularly scheduled meetings of the board, local school improvement councils, parent-teacher organizations, booster clubs, principal, area administrative teams, faculty senates, and employee representatives.

Students usually have less access to this "meeting" communication vehicle. The establishment of two additional communication vehicle requirements improves this avenue for receiving and giving information for students. First, student advisors should be required in all high schools. Student/teacher advisors provide a mandatory key link between students and staff and enhance opportunities for students to get answers to questions and to express concern on any issue. It also provides a structured opportunity for other constituent groups—building and office staff, management team, board, and community—to receive information pertaining

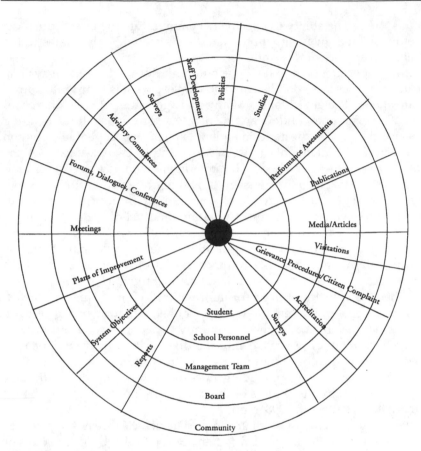

FIGURE 2.2 Continuous Communication Synergy Cycle

to student concerns. Second, annual meetings between the superintendent, members of the management team, and secondary students should be scheduled at least once a year in each high school. A representative sample of students in each high school should be asked to meet with the superintendent, members of the management team, building principal, and faculty senate president. Students' suggestions, concerns, and recommendations should be taken seriously. Reform initiatives and the subsequent defined system and work objectives need to be based on student recommendations in each of the high schools. Students need updated on progress relating to the previous year's recommendations at annual student/management meetings.

The application of the communication Synergy Cycle Model in a school system is helpful in analyzing gaps in communication vehicles. The following briefly explains each of the vehicles listed in the synergy cycle model. If a school system demonstrates that communication avenues are in place, it then becomes the responsibility of those desiring to receive or acquire information to utilize the applicable vehicle. Evidence of appropriate communication vehicles for each constituency group, such as those listed in the Synergy Cycle Model, in a school system reduces the "I didn't know—I wasn't involved" phenomenon that often derails operational and improvement activities.

COMMUNICATION VEHICLES

Reports

Annual Reports

Each year a compilation of pertinent statistical and factual information regarding school and school system progress needs to be compiled into a publishable annual report document. This report should be published as an insert in all local newspapers and distributed to all students, staff, parents, and the business community. The annual report should be made easy to read and interesting to the public through human interest features and pictures and lists of specific accomplishments of schools, staff, students, parents, and community members.

Board Reports

A significant number and type of various reports need to routinely flow to the board. Each week boards should be provided a document entitled Board Report. The Board Report should provide narrative summaries of progress on specific programs, services or operational area. The contents of the Board Report may vary from week to week but generally contains the following items:

1. Calendar of events occurring within the district;
2. Board agenda items and supporting information;
3. Status of legislative initiatives;
4. Summaries of pending or on-going legal cases;
5. Recommendations for modifications of regulations/policies; and
6. Subject/issue reports on such topics as violence, drugs, alternative schools, summer school, alternative schools, centralized food service, and so on.

7. Summaries of out-of-county travel requests;
8. Requests for funds on special projects: Title I, vocational education, Head-Start, Eisenhower Project, and so on;
9. Meeting agendas and reports for any organization for which a
   board member or superintendent represents the school system;
10. Audit reports; and
11. Special concern summaries of progress or concerns as they relate
    to implementation of a particular initiative; such as full-day
    kindergarten, relocating of special needs students to their home
    school, establishment of a new comprehensive student data base,
    and so on.

Superintendent Activity Report

The board should also receive a weekly document entitled Superintendent's Activity Report that summarizes the major activities/occurrences
that had the superintendent's direct attention during the week. This con-
fidential report is designed to help the board understand the current
issues, concerns, and tasks. The Superintendent's Activity Report should
assist board members when they receive a call from a concerned citizen
regarding specific issues that may have escalated during the week. The
report will also give the board a greater understanding of the complexity
operation within the school system.

Reports at Board Meetings

Reports should be a standing category on regular board agendas used
regularly to disseminate comprehensive summaries on specific projects,
subjects, or initiatives. Administrators should prepare these reports to
educate board members and the public on specific topics. Reports can be
requested by the board or suggested by the administration. Board members should utilize the report section of board agendas to request information on issues that are escalating in terms of public concern. Boards
should schedule the administration's report for a board meeting at least
one month after a request for information is made. This delay provides
time to communicate to the public that a report will be made at a future
board meeting and time for administration to adequately prepare for a
public report. Routine progress reports should also be scheduled on all
initiatives that occur in the school system. Reports might address any or
all of the following subject areas: finance, personnel, instruction, special
education, vocational education, secondary restructuring initiative, inclusion, multi-age grouping, block scheduling, drugs, violence, discipline,

attendance, maintenance, transportation, research, staffing, system objectives, organizational structure, administrative personnel, salaries, facilities, federal programs, food service, purchasing, distribution, custodial services, staff development, cultural diversity, community relations, school effectiveness inventory, community survey results, information systems, communications, alternative schools, homebound education, home-school education, preschool and kindergarten programs, music and art services, nursing services, social services, and so on. Board requests for reports on topics of interest require adjustment to administrators' schedules to accommodate a board-imposed timeline for completion. Although it is an excellent avenue for keeping the board and public informed, the time invested in this report vehicle can be enormous.

System Objectives

The development of annual system objectives is a process that involves every constituency group and enhances communication opportunities at all levels. A first step in development of system objectives is determining need based on statistical and factual data. This data is collected from students, employees, management team, and community. The system objective process provides many opportunities for involvement that enhance communication. The need process, the development of objectives and activities, the dissemination of information about system initiatives, and the evaluation of the success of each objective all provide opportunities for receiving and giving information from all constituent groups. Other vehicles, such as surveys, meetings, conferences, and forums, are used to collect necessary input in determining the system objectives. The system objectives should be communicated to all constituent groups. Meetings, conferences, forums, publications, and the media are used to communicate and implement the defined objectives. Performance assessment communication vehicle is utilized to determine the effectiveness and level of implementation of each objective. (The system objective development process is discussed in detail in Chapter 3.)

Plans of Improvement

Plans of improvement are documents required at all levels of operation: building, department, and central office. Plans of improvement require extensive communication with all affected entities. For example, at the school level, representative staff, student, parent, and community need to be involved in all components of developing, implementing, and evaluating plans of improvement. Plans of improvement define specific needs, state objectives for remedy, elaborate activities to be implemented, and outline a standard for determining improvement. Each school should use statistical and factual data (attendance, grades, standardized test scores, effectiveness inventories, graduation rate, and so on) to determine needs. Once needs are established, faculty representatives, local school improvement council representatives, and the principal should define specific objectives to be addressed during the school year. Activities necessary to achieve the objectives should be defined. Plans of improvement should be approved by the local school improvement council (LSIC) and the faculty senate and are submitted to the area assistant superintendent and the management team. Local school improvement plans should be used to generate factual and statistical information for developing system objectives in a comprehensive county education improvement plan. The submission of local improvement plans enhances and coordinates consistency at all levels through improved continuous communication.

To develop the county education improvement plan, an advisory committee consisting of representatives from business and the community, parents, employees, and students should be established. The committee should provide input and approve of the comprehensive county education improvement, and affirm that the plan reflects local needs. The county education improvement plan should also be submitted to the board for review and approval.

Meetings

The community generally has excellent opportunities to attend board meetings to express concerns, make recommendations, or listen to information on system initiatives, plans, programs, and services. Most boards hold both regular and special meetings that are open for community attendance. Delegations are usually accepted at some time during board meetings. Board meetings, as a vehicle for communication, ensure sufficient opportunity for community input and are an important source of information regarding activities within the system.

The community should provide and receive information by participating in local school improvement councils (LSIC). LSICs should be established in each school and require community representation. Most major documents should require review by the LSIC: plans of improvement, budgets, and safe schools plan. Community members should also be solicited to participate in parent-teacher organizations and/or booster clubs.

Board meetings provide opportunities for staff at the building and central office level to interact with the board. Regular and special board meetings should be utilized as a vehicle for good communication with employees.

Employees on the management team, representing departments, offices, and schools, are provided a multitude of opportunities within the meeting vehicle to receive and give information:

- Management team meetings held monthly with representatives from elementary/secondary principal associations and teacher associations;
- Department and office meetings held at least monthly;
- Area meetings with principals, support personnel held monthly;
- Faculty senate staff meetings for all teachers/support personnel and building administrators held monthly;
- Employee organization representatives meet monthly with the superintendent; and
- Special projects (Title I, exceptional children, and so on) require meetings with schools and community members.

A regular schedule of advisory–student meetings be established in all secondary schools. The superintendent should also meet annually with a representative group of students in each high school. Meeting with secondary students with the superintendent, principal, faculty senate president, and area assistant superintendent are important vehicles to enhance communication and bring about system improvement. Students need the opportunity to express concerns and make recommendations. It is important for changes resulting from student recommendations to be communicated back to the students in the student newsletter published by the school system.

Each school should be expected to establish new and maintain existing vehicles to receive and give information with students, such as student councils and club meetings. Secondary schools should also establish regular dialogue meetings with fifteen to twenty randomly selected students who and the principal and teacher department chairs.

Forums/Dialogues/Conferences

Special forums, dialogues, and conferences are communication vehicles that should be used to receive and give information when initiatives, concerns, issues, and tasks arise. Forums, dialogues, and conferences should be held to (1) disseminate knowledge and information on the issue; (2) provide opportunity for constituent groups to express concern; and (3) design recommendations for the system to consider and implement. Conferences provide an opportunity to communicate with representative segments of a variety of constituent groups: students, schools, teachers, service personnel, community members, and business and government leaders. Major initiatives and/or project requirements often serve as the catalyst for conferences on such topics as cultural diversity, peer coaching, and drug education.

Boards should establish dialogues with constituent groups—parents, service personnel, teachers, and administrators—to hear concerns and recommendations. No formal action should be taken in board forums or dialogues. Because most school districts are faced with facility issues, board dialogues or forums on this topic can effectively initiate discussion about declining facilities and public support for needed renovations/maintenance.

Advisory Committees

Advisory committees are important communication vehicles that should be standard in school districts. They should provide review, approval, and on-going counsel for any initiative, major task, or issue that must be addressed. Advisory committees provide a structured opportunity to receive and give information from each constituent group. Without review by an established advisory committee, most new initiatives are doomed. The superintendent, as well as projects and program initiatives, should have advisory committees:

- Superintendent Advisory Committee
- Exceptional Children Advisory Committee
- Title One Advisory Committee
- Vocational Education Advisory Committee
- School to Work Advisory Committee
- Secondary School Restructuring Advisory Committee
- Information Systems Advisory Committee
- Transportation Advisory Committee
- Personnel Advisory Committee
- Maintenance Advisory Committee
- Drug Education Advisory Committee
- County Education Plan Advisory Committee

Surveys

Major initiatives should be predated by surveys that justified the initiative. Comprehensive community surveys are beneficial but sometimes controversial. The cost and time spent conducting surveys are often criticized. However, information garnered from a general survey of the community and staff can be instrumental for securing their buy-in for specific initiatives and objectives that are based on needs identified within the survey results.

Employee surveys help determine needs and subsequent system and work objectives. It is important that a significant number of employees return the survey so that results appropriately reflect the workforce.

Surveys generated by organizations outside the system can be problematic. Outside surveys may lack correct technical design, proper distribution of instrument, low response of returns, and publication of results if they are too few respondents. There needs to be a process for approving all surveys, both internal and external, that are to be used in a school system. The process needs to include a review by administration to ensure the survey's applicability to the system's vision and mission and review by the research department to determine technical correctness. School effectiveness inventories are probably one of the best examples of a structured survey that provides a great deal of important information ascertained from all constituent groups. School effectiveness inventories, administered at least every two years, should be based on state standards, school district minimum requirements and system objectives. School systems should invest in the necessary research to develop an effectiveness inventory survey that would assess the various constituent groups: students, teachers, parents, and service personnel regarding major aspects of school operation. An acceptable performance rating should be established and utilized for evaluating school effectiveness and determining areas for improvement. The results of the school effectiveness survey should be reflected in the school improvement plan and, subsequently, the county improvement plan. (See Appendix C for Kanawha County Schools' Effective Schools Inventory.)

Community Education and Staff Development

Community education and staff development training are important communication vehicles for giving and receiving information from all constituent groups. Staff development can be controversial because of the commitment of time and money required for its successful implementation. Structured staff development opportunities should be in place, and educational programs that support knowledge and understanding of the school system should be in place for the community.

Board members should receive a variety of articles and reports in a weekly report designed to increase knowledge and understanding of the school system needs, operation, and best education practices. Informational reports should also be a component of all board meetings. The informational reports or presentations should increase board and community understanding of concerns and issues pertinent to public education. Informational reports should be at the top of board agendas so as to: (1) acknowledge their importance; (2) ensure greater dissemination of information to the public; and (3) increase the board's understanding of the subject.

A variety of educational opportunities should be available to community members. First, the community should receive information from reports presented at board meetings and through such avenues as school system press releases, newspaper articles, television newscasts, and, if possible, through a school system television station. Second, training sessions should be scheduled to enhance effective parent and community participation in LSICs. Local school improvement councils should be in place in all schools, and representatives who serve on this council should be knowledgeable about the school system and interested in securing the best educational opportunities for children. Schedule training to LSIC representatives on such topics as role and responsibilities, system objectives, education issues, and school system funding. Third, system-wide conferences on important topics should include representation from local school improvement councils and at times be open to the general community. Fourth, county resource centers for parents of exceptional children should be established to provide structured opportunities for increasing parent understanding and skills. Fifth, family resource centers should be established in various geographical locations in the county to help parents develop good parenting skills, find necessary support services, and enhance their knowledge and understanding of student performance standards. A variety of programs, services, and training opportunities should be made available to parents through the family resource centers. Sixth, specific special-funded projects such as Title One, vocational education, Head Start, drug education, and safe schools, should include parental/community education activities.

Staff development should be comprehensive, on-going, and supported by increased dollars to local schools earmarked for more and better training opportunities. All schools, offices, and departments should be provided a minimum of one day per month of paid staff development. Additional pre- and postschool staff development days are also essential. Employees should determine staff development needs and incorporate the activities into the school improvement plan. The county should provide adequate funding and support for appropriate staff development in each school. All school, department, and county improvement plans should delineate specific opportunities for staff development. County staff development initiatives should support school-wide staff training on appropriate instructional strategies and should review school needs and the development of plans of actions to bring about school improvement. All elementary and secondary schools should have week-long staff development opportunities at least once every three years. Evidence of comprehensive staff development opportunities at all operational levels should be included in the county annual report.

Policies

To ensure appropriate opportunities for communication, the process for policy development must ask for input from all constituent groups. The development of a new policy or the revision of an existing policy requires adherence to a prescribed process that assures all constituent groups have opportunity for input over a reasonable period of time. The process should entail initial discussion at a board meeting, with no action required, of all new or proposed revisions of policies. If no additional major changes to the proposed policy are recommended, the draft policy should be distributed for comment to all school personnel and to faculty senates and local school improvement councils. The policy should be submitted to the superintendent's advisory committee for review and comment. The process of review should be a one- to two-month process, depending on the ability to adequately distribute it and sufficient time for response. All comments and suggestions should be returned to the board for final consideration, approval, or rejection. The development of policy and the opportunity for input is the board's primary function. All counties must have a policy outlining the process for policy development. The following components should be apparent in all board policies that prescribe the process for policy development:.

- *Opportunity for Employee and Public Involvement:* Policy reflects encouragement to all persons or groups to communicate to the superintendent any perceived need for the development of new policy or a change of existing policy for consideration. Public is encouraged to provide comment at board meetings on proposed policies or changes to existing policies.
- *Review by Advisory Committee:* Policy proposals and changes reviewed by the superintendent's advisory committee. (Established advisory committee consisting of representatives from all employee groups in the school system.) Superintendent's advisory committee prepares a report on each policy reviewed and sends it to the board for consideration. The report contains the following items:
  a. Recommendation for approval, approval with reservations, or disapproval;
  b. Suggested changes to proposed policy;
  c. Determination of possible fiscal impact; and
  d. Dissenting views and comments of committee members.

- *Public Comment:* All policy proposals are placed on first reading at a regularly scheduled meeting. No action on the proposed policy is taken until the next regularly scheduled meeting. Between the time a proposal is placed on first reading and the following regularly scheduled board meeting, the superintendent accepts written comments upon the merits of policy proposals. A summary of written comments is provided to the board prior to any second reading vote.
- *Invitation to Comment/Faculty Senates and School Improvement Councils:* A proposed policy or change shall be distributed to faculty senates and local school improvement councils for review and comment. Comments are sent to board members.

This policy development and/or modification process is an important communication vehicle. In-depth understanding of the board's role as a policy-maker is critical to the board's success. Policy-making is the key role of boards. Understanding this primary role and the defined policy process that ensures the board's effectiveness as a policy-making entity is critical if boards are to stay focused on their role and responsibilities, including communication opportunities.

Studies

A study meant to address a specific concern or initiative is an important communication vehicle for securing factual information and obtaining a broad range of input. Studies are perhaps an underutilized vehicle in most school systems because of three hindrances: (1) individuals with specific expertise may not be willing to serve on the study committee because of the amount of time required; (2) studies are time-consuming and can be costly if substitutes are required to cover for teachers/ administrators who serve on the committee; and (3) there can be a notion that studies are used to delay action and that recommendations from completed studies are seldom acted on. People may worry that a controversy may evolve if recommendations are implemented.

The strength, knowledge, and commitment of constituency represented on the study committee will determine if the committee's recommendation(s) are implemented. By verifying that representatives from all constituencies are involved and that a broad audience has the opportunity for input in the process of study, potential unrest and controversy is lessened. For example, a superintendent might consider organizing a "business" study. Because school systems are often the most important "business" in the community, the efficiency and effectiveness of the system's business operations are extremely important to the financial condition of the school district. Accounting, purchasing, information systems, operations, maintenance, finance, food service, personnel, and communication are departments found in most school districts as well as the business and industrial community. A study commissioned by the superintendent that brings together leaders from the business community, such as CEOs from industry and business, to study all aspects of business operation in the school district is productive for a number of reasons:

1. It improves communication and understanding between the business and education communities. For example, business representatives will gain a clearer understanding of federal and state requirements that restrict school systems from operating in ways that are considered best in the business sector.
2. It brings together experts who work in business and industry without cost to the school system to review a variety of the system's business and operational functions. These contacts can be continued long after the study is completed. These experts may be willing to serve as advisors or members of advisory committees for specific departments.
3. Recommendations for change may be developed that could result in cost savings or increase efficiency.

Performance Assessments

Performance assessments are a necessary component to evaluate progress in most school organizations and are important communication vehicles as well. Assessment instruments garner information related to student and employees performance. Standardized test measures provide factual information on the academic achievement of all students in the school system. Quantitative information that can be garnered by effectively analyzing test results is fundamental to school system operation. The Stanford Achievement Test, SAT, and ACT, are examples of instruments that provide detailed information on how well students perform and identify specific strengths and weaknesses. Test information justifies needed change or improvement. Comparison of local student's performance with scores in the state and nation are often published in local newspapers. The publishing of the school district's performance on standardized test measures communicates to the public how well the school district is doing in relation to other districts. In some school districts individual school performance on standardized test measures is published in the newspaper.

Employee evaluations are excellent tools to communicate how the employee's performance level relates to prescribed standards. The system's priorities can be incorporated into evaluation performance objectives in individual teacher and administrators' professional development plans for the year. Routine revision of employee evaluation instruments to ensure they reflect the priorities and expectations of the school system is essential.

Effective school inventories or surveys, as discussed in previous sections, are examples of assessment instruments designed to ascertain the opinion of each constituent group about the school and school system progress. Inventory assessments provide valuable information on the opinions of students, teachers, service personnel, administrators and parents regarding their school and school system. Results of the effective school inventories should be communicated to all constituent groups and utilized in the school improvement process.

Publications

School system publications should distribute information to each constituent group. With adequate distribution and constituent interest, these publications are excellent communication vehicle. The following are types of publications that should be regularly produced and distributed by the school system:

- *Annual Report:* The annual report should be compiled annually to communicate information regarding individual student, teacher, school, and school system accomplishments. The annual report should be in newspaper format that is easily read. The report should be distributed to every student, teacher, school improvement council, and government and business leader, and be inserted into the major newspapers for community distribution.
- *Employee Publication:* An employee publication is designed for employees to share successes and to increase communication with the workforce about events, issues, programs, services, and accomplishments. The publication should also be circulated to business, government leaders, and LSICs to communicate information on issues, major tasks, initiatives, and curriculum projects accomplished by the district. The publication should contain many of the following sections: superintendent's message, calendar information, staff development programs, and accomplishments of personnel, the school, and the system. The publication should be distributed monthly and

feature stories with pictures should make this publication easily read and of interest to everyone.

- *Student Publication:* A magazine written by students and published either in conjunction with a local newspaper or by the school system's department of communication should be published at least on a quarterly basis. Students from all high schools should contribute articles of interest for publication. Students, events, issues, and accomplishments are the focus of this publication. It should feature summaries of the superintendent's annual meeting with high school students.

- *Student Handbook:* At the beginning of each school year, students in each school must receive a student handbook containing specific information pertaining to each individual school, including the mission and vision statement, staff, course offerings, schedules, fees, and attendance requirements. The handbook should contain student behavior policy, notification of Title IX Grievance Procedure, special education and 504 referral process, and drug and alcohol policies. Schools compile their own handbook to help both students and parents find necessary information about each school's rules, regulations, and expectations.

- *Employee Handbook:* Each school should publish an employee handbook containing basic information about the school and school system, information on the school and county calendar, attendance procedures, grading procedures, work hours, services available in the school, purchasing, travel requirements, grievance procedures, sexual harassment notification requirements, student discipline and attendance forms, fire and emergency evacuation procedures, and teacher code of conduct. The teachers' handbook is designed to be a guide for pertinent information about school and county procedures.

- *Brochures:* A multitude of brochures should be published each year and distributed to students, teachers, parents, and the community. They include: "The Results Are In," an accomplishment brochure containing statistical information about the school system; "A School System Soaring Higher," an accomplishment brochure highlighting specific program accomplishments; "Higher Standards," outlining specific standards and expectations that must be met by each student; "What Will My Child Learn in School," a parent's guide to student performance standards in elementary, middle, and high school; "Community Alliances to Support Education," outlining guidelines for establishing and maintaining partnerships between schools and business/industry; "Solving Problems Brochure," designed to address parents' specific school concerns. Brochures should be routinely developed to explain specific new initiatives, outline specific program requirements, and acquaint the public with specific projects, such as Title I, special education, and vocational education. There should be an expectation that all departments routinely develop brochures with prescribed distributions to help communicate pertinent information regarding programs and services.

Media/Articles

The communication department should weekly provide the media with a press release covering upcoming events, issues, programs, and services of interest. The news release contains notification of calendar events in the school system for the upcoming week. Special news releases should be generated by the communication department when a specific crisis or newsworthy event occurs. Frequent news releases generate a multitude of special interest stories.

The media frequently conducts their own investigations of "leads" provided by parents, community members, staff, and board members. The communication department should routinely develop informational press releases to provide factual information and clarification regarding subjects the media is investigating.

A school system television channel is an excellent vehicle for communication to all constituent groups. Television shows should be designed by students, teachers, and administrators and regularly feature special programs, services, and schools. Some television programs should be designed entirely by students and feature only students. Area assistant superintendents should be responsible for designing shows that feature schools within their attendance area. Specific feature programs are designed to explain given initiatives, such as bonds, levies, comprehensive education facility plans, secondary restructuring, Orff music, full-day kindergarten, community service, family resource centers, sexual harassment, smoking and drugs, discipline procedures, alternative schools, staff development, and special education.

A school system television station may also be utilized to broadcast tapes of the regular board meetings. Live call-in shows with board members and the superintendent are beneficial because they provide an opportunity to listen to community concerns and to direct calls to appropriate personnel to resolve.

Visitations

A structured visitation program should be in place in each school. Parents, teachers, administrators, senior citizens, and business and community members should be encouraged to visit schools. Schools should hold open houses for the community members, establish grandparents and senior-citizen days, and offer senior-citizen lunch programs. Senior-citizens involvement in schools encourages support from a population who do not have children in school and are an opportunity to dispel negative perceptions of schools. High school students should visit other schools as well. A student exchange program strengthens school relationships and gives participants a glimpse of what actually happens in another school. Teachers and administrators should be encouraged to visit other schools and surrounding school districts that have specific programs/services of interest.

Moving central office administrators and support personnel to schools increases their visibility and helps them become very familiar with what is happening in each building. Central office administrators, including the superintendent, should be expected to substitute teach a minimum of three days in schools. When the central office provides classroom coverage, teachers and administrators can visit other schools without incurring additional substitute cost. Superintendent and administrative staff should make unscheduled and frequent school visits. Frequent visitations provide for a greater understanding of what is needed in today's schools.

Grievance/Citizen Complaint Procedures

The grievance and citizen complaint process should be stipulated in board policy and distributed to all employees. Formal procedures for addressing unresolved problems need to be in place in all school districts. Although people tend to think of a grievance procedure negatively, it is an organized, structured process designed to help employees and students address concerns/problems and receive definitive answers to their questions. Substantial efforts are made to make students and employees knowledgeable of their rights and responsibilities. The grievance process should afford opportunity to be heard at various levels: building or department, superintendent, board, outside the system grievance board, and then the courts. In addition, a citizen complaint process needs to be established for parents who believe their concern or problem is not adequately addressed. The citizen complaint process includes opportunity for the superintendent's designee to listen to the complaint and render a decision.

COMMUNICATION SUMMARY

"To overcome the major burden of proving that organizational change was effectively communicated, change initiatives must shift significant responsibility for understanding back to those receiving the information about change" (Patterson 1997, 15). Everyone has a natural tendency to profess confusion about change, and the superintendent must implement strategies to determine if everyone receives the information associated with the proposed change. The application of the "continuous communication synergy cycle" to determine if sufficient communication vehicles are in place is a good exercise to identify communication deficiencies in a school district. Once appropriate vehicles for communication are in place, the excuses for not knowing or not being involved can be dramatically reduced or eliminated. Communication vehicles must serve all constituent groups and, in a variety of ways and processes, support an effective management system.

Superintendents should have an open-door policy as an informal way to receive information. However, without an organized, systematic way of receiving regular input and a method of assessing communication opportunities, the likelihood of addressing the communication needs of a complex school system diminishes.

The superintendent is the leader of a school system communication network. It is extremely important for the superintendent to clearly set forth expectations for communication vehicles. This level of expectation must be filtered throughout the system. The management team's guiding principles, priorities, and expectations are the core components of any opportunity to communicate with the administration's various constituents. Setting expectations is not to be confused with being an autocratic leader who gives out commands, controls decisions, and is ultimately responsible for all successes and failures. Quite the contrary, the democratic leader of an educational system is committed to communicating that all of us are dedicated to achieving what "we" believe is good for children. Communicating each individual's ownership and responsibility to achieve what is best for children is the important message.

MANAGEMENT SYSTEM SUMMARY

An effective management system that is understood and supported by the board is imperative to system success. Board understanding and support needs to be wholehearted and long term. A one- or two-year commitment to a method of organization is not sufficient. A well-thought out administrative organization and management system needs to be established at the beginning of the superintendent's term. However, long-term commitment should be supported by an administrative requirement to provide data to demonstrate progress in predetermined indicators.

An effective management system has the following well-defined elements: (1) administrative organization structure that ensures a high level of accountability at every operational level through reasonable supervisory ratios and supports site-based management; (2) defined principles and priorities that reflect an understanding of the board's vision; (3) defined improvement process that includes the development of annual system, work objectives, and a comprehensive evaluation report; and (4) comprehensive communication system that includes a method to validate number and types of opportunities to receive and provide information. Boards and superintendents who understand and support a management system with these defined elements operate school systems that are more likely to achieve a high level of efficiency and that demonstrate school and system progress.

A third essential component for making school systems work is the establishment of a structured improvement process. Chapter 3 describes a system improvement process designed to bring about progress at the school and system level and is replicable in most school districts.

CHAPTER 3

System Improvement Process: "Laying New Track"

One of the greatest barriers to lasting change in schools . . . is the
fact that few district offices and few communities have developed the capacity to encourage, support and sustain change in
classroom and in schools.

—PHILLIP C. SCHLECTY, *INVENTING BETTER SCHOOLS*

INTRODUCTION

A clearly defined system improvement process is essential for bringing
about school system improvement, or "laying new track." Boards should
understand the importance of the process, hold the administration
accountable for implementing an improvement plan at every level of
operation, and require annual demonstration and evaluation of progress.
This chapter delineates an improvement process that can be replicated in
school districts.

The system improvement process described in this chapter includes
requirements for input from all constituency groups; analysis of statistical information, including standardized test scores, drop-out rate, graduation rate, discipline data, attendance data, effectiveness inventories and
community surveys; and submission of required project, department,
school, and district improvement plans and evaluation reports. Five
defined areas for system improvement are established: (1) instruction; (2)
communication; (3) finance; (4) operations; and (5) facilities. System
objectives address each improvement area designation. System objectives
are data-driven, based on needs assessment conclusions and focused on
improvement of student learning and achievement.

The system improvement process defined in this chapter includes
four important components: establishment of a common foundation; definition of a needs assessment process; development of system (focus and

work) objectives; and determination of accountability measures. In addition, the school system improvement process requires involvement and implementation at every level of operation.

The first component of the system improvement process is the importance of establishing a common foundation on which to develop improvement plans. Each school district should determine foundational considerations. Four examples of foundational considerations are provided: school effectiveness correlates; ten key practices from High Schools That Work; and state board policy delineating standards and minimum organizational structure requirements.

A second component of the system improvement process is establishment of a needs assessment. Determination of need should be based on statistical and factual information garnered from schools, offices, departments, the management team, board, and community. Need should be established for at least the following areas within a school system: Instruction, communication, finance, operations, and facilities. For the purposes of discussing the construction of a needs assessment, the five areas have been regrouped into three comprehensive areas: instruction, operations (which includes finance and communication), and facilities. Examples of statistical and factual information compiled and analyzed in the needs assessment process are defined for each area.

The third component of a system improvement process addresses the development of system objectives. Focus and work objectives are developed in five areas: instruction, communication, finance, operations, and facilities.

The fourth component of an improvement process determines the strategies used to ensure accountability at each level of operation. Suggested monitoring requirements are provided. Examples of anticipated accomplishments that should result from the system improvement process are offered.

FOUNDATIONAL CONSIDERATIONS
FOR SYSTEM IMPROVEMENT

School Effectiveness Correlates

Research supports the importance of school effectiveness correlates in achieving school improvement. Understanding of the correlates helps determine need and subsequent objective development within the school and system improvement process. School effectiveness correlates should be reflected in school and county improvement plans. The application of correlates to school data reveals areas of strengths and weaknesses. Utilizing the effectiveness correlates as a standard determines areas of need that should be addressed in the improvement process. Staff development programs should be designed to assist project, department, and school administrators with understanding school effectiveness correlates.

The correlates should also be incorporated into personnel evaluations and professional development plans. School effectiveness inventories or surveys should be initiated that evaluate student, staff, and parent perception of the school's success as it relates to each school effectiveness correlate (see Appendix C). Effectiveness surveys provide essential information for determining need for the improvement process. Table 3.1 summarizes the school effectiveness correlates that are recommended as a foundational consideration for school improvement processes.

High Schools That Work—Ten Key Practices

Schools and central office need to study the ten key practices for effective schools, identified in High Schools That Work literature, as a foundation for developing improvement plans. The ten key practices are applicable to comprehensive K–12 instructional improvement efforts. Table 3.2 lists Bottoms' ten key practices of high schools that work. After receiving comprehensive training in High Schools That Work strategies, the management team should utilize these strategies for assisting schools in the development of their individual school improvement plans (Bottoms, Presson, and Johnson 1992, 6).

State Standards

Consideration of the state's critical program elements or standards at every level of operation is essential for school and school district success, compliance with state accreditation requirements, and development of effective improvement plans. Most state departments of education delineate standards that local school districts need to address. The standards are usually defined in policy and determined through research and practice to be critical to the operation of a successful school system. State

TABLE 3.1   School Effectiveness Correlates

1.	Clear and focused mission
2.	Positive learning climate
3.	Strong instructional leadership
4.	High expectations for student success
5.	Student time on task
6.	Monitoring student progress
7.	Effective home/school relations

Lezotte 1991, 1

TABLE 3.2   10 Key Practices of High Schools That Work

1.	High expectations are established in schools and classrooms.
2.	Vocational teachers insist their students use academic content.
3.	Academic teachers use more engaging and applied learning strategies in teaching higher-level academic content to students.
4.	Students complete a challenging program of study with an upgraded core and a major.
5.	Students are provided access to a structured system of work-based learning.
6.	Academic and vocational teachers work together to plan challenging activities that cause students to use complex academic skills.
7.	Students are actively engaged in the learning process by making learning more active and less passive.
8.	Guidance and advisement process are strengthened through getting teachers and parents involved in the effort.
9.	Students are provided a structured system of extra help and time to achieve higher standards.
10.	Score is maintained on what is working and what is not working, eliminating things that no longer work, and adopting activities that do work.

Bottoms, Presson, and Johnson 1992, 6

standards should be addressed within local schools and school districts improvement plans. States usually define standards in a variety of areas including curriculum or instruction, finance, transportation, alternative education, school–community relations, personnel, staff development, student performance, administration, and facilities. School districts should institute local policy and procedures to ensure compliance with each state standard. Each school system should review state standards and require schools to develop their improvement plans after careful consideration of the standards. It is important that improvement processes at every level of operation consider state standards when determining need and developing appropriate objectives.

Minimum Organizational Requirements

Consideration of minimum organization requirements is intrinsic to effective improvement processes. Minimum requirements need to be clearly defined, articulated, and agreed upon by sectors of the educational community: boards, superintendent, administrators, teachers, and service personnel. Each school district needs to develop a comprehensive document that lists agreed-upon minimum organizational requirements for personnel and programs. The improvement process may be delayed and even derailed for a period if comprehensive minimum organizational requirements are not in place. Personnel and programmatic requirements serve as a standard to measure what exists against what should exist. Minimum organizational requirements provide a common purpose and direction for the school system and are a fundamental starting point for an improvement process in schools and school districts.

NEEDS ASSESSMENT

The second component in the improvement process is the establishment of need. The need assessment process should include an evaluation of foundational considerations determined to be essential to school and school district success. Schools and school districts should utilize defined foundational considerations, such as school effectiveness correlates, ten key practices for High Schools That Work, state standards or critical elements, and minimal organizational requirements to measure what exists against what *should* exist. The need assessment requires careful analysis of pertinent data against the foundational considerations in order to determine defined areas of need. Factual and statistical data should be utilized to establish need in three broad categories: instruction, operation (which includes communication and finance), and facilities.

Instruction

School profiles should provide a comprehensive summary of pertinent statistical and factual data. Central office administration should annually develop these profiles to ensure consistency in review of specified data and to reduce each school's workload in compiling needs assessment data. The school profiles should include basic demographic information, standardized test scores, grade summaries, drop-out and graduation rates, suspension, attendance, and school staffing. Table 3.3 defines the specific categories of information that should be provided to individual schools. Depending on the school and school district requirements, specific data categories may need to be deleted or added. It is important that schools understand how the data in the school profile is determined. An accompanying definition of school profile statistical terms should be available.

Table 3.4 defines terms utilized in the school profile, which is a quick reference on numerous performance categories that are beneficial in determining school effectiveness and need. To determine growth or need in specific performance categories, school profiles should be kept over a period of time. Utilization of school profiles ensures a common set of data is analyzed in determining need. District-developed school profiles assist

TABLE 3.3   School Profiles

Demographics

Accreditation status
Grade range
Second month enrollment
Minority enrollment(%)
Student mobility(%)
Free and reduced lunch (%)
Abuse and vandalism ($)
Student attendance
Promotion rate
Retention rate
Average class size
Pupil-teacher ratio
Instructional costs per pupil ($)
Satisfaction with school (%)

Standardized Achievement Testing

Grade 3, 6, 9, and/or 11
Reading %ile rank
Language %ile rank
Mathematics %ile rank
Basic Skills %ile rank
Percent scoring above 50%ile in basic skills
Percent scoring below 40%ile in basic skills

ACT/SAT Testing Results

Percent Taking ACT
ACT English
ACT Mathematics
ACT Reading
ACT Scientific Reasoning
ACT Composite
Percent Taking SAT
SAT Verbal
SAT Mathematics

Honors Classes and Grades

Percent of students enrolled in Honors classes
Percent As
Percent Bs
Percent Cs

Grade Distribution—Regular Classes
Percent As
Percent Bs
Percent Cs
Percent below C

Other Performance Indicators
Suspensions to student affairs
Drug and alcohol suspensions
Graduation rate
Drop-out rate

School Staffing
Principal/assistant principal
Counselors
Librarians
Classroom and classroom support teachers
Special education teachers
Service staff

Staff Attendance
Principal/assistant principal
Counselors
Librarians
Classroom and classroom support teachers
Special education teachers
Service staff

Kanawha County Schools

schools in maintaining and summarizing data for need analysis within the school improvement process. Table 3.5 provides data on a fictitious high school utilizing school profile data.

School principals and central office administrators should analyze the school data profiles together with staff to determine areas that require attention or improvement. School profile data provides an excellent starting point to analyze need in specific schools and at the district level. The management team should review all schools' profiles to determine general trends of strengths and weaknesses within the district.

Additional data may also need to be considered. For example, a school district may determine that a survey of graduates is beneficial in

TABLE 3.4   Definition of School Profile Terms

Second month enrollment	The number of enrolled students at end of the second month of school
Student attendance rate	The average daily attendance for students, determined by dividing total number of days present by total number of membership days
Promotion rate	Determined by dividing total number of students promoted by total net enrollment
Retention rate	Determined by dividing total number of students retained by total net enrollment
Drop-out rate	Determined by dividing number of drop-outs by the number of drop-outs plus graduates
Graduation rate	Determined by dividing number of graduates by the number of 9th-graders enrolled four years prior
School satisfaction	The combined percentage of students, parents, and professional staff who express satisfaction with their school (School Effectiveness Inventory)
Standardized test results	The percentile ranks in reading, language, mathematics, and basic skills that indicate average students' performance on each subtest. The percentage of students scoring above the 50th percentile shows the proportion of students in the upper quartiles. The percent scoring below the 40th percentile is an indicator of the academic need.
Minority enrollment (%)	Percentage of student enrollment that is nonwhite.
Free and reduced lunch (%)	The percentage of students receiving free or reduced lunch rates
Student mobility (%)	Student mobility is determined by dividing transfers in plus transfers out by second month enrollment
Average class size	The average number of students in a regular education classroom receiving instruction in English/language arts, mathematics, science, and social studies
Pupil-teacher ratio	Determined by dividing total number of students by total number of full-time equivalent teachers

Kanawha County Schools

TABLE 3.5 Fictitious High School Profile

Fictitious High School	1999-00	1998-99	1997-98
Demographics			
Accreditation status	Full	Full	Full
Grade range	10–12	10–12	10–12
Second month enrollment	1,253	1,233	1,312
Minority enrollment (%)	27.7%	22.4%	23.8%
Student mobility (%)	15.8%	25.6%	23.6%
Free and reduced lunch (%)	25.9%	32.8%	24.7%
Abuse and vandalism ($)	$7,691	$4,871	$1,742
Student attendance	91.8%	98.6%	93.8%
Average class size	19	23.5	27.9
Pupil-teacher ratio	15.3	14.9	14.2
Instructional cost per pupil ($	$4,354	$4,534	$4,315
Satisfaction with school (%)	90.6%	90.6%	80.2%
Standardized Testing			
Grade	11	11	11
Reading %ile rank	61	58	62
Language %ile rank	65	53	60
Mathematics %ile rank	63	56	63
Basic Skills %ile rank	63	56	62
% Above 50%ile basic skills	68.6%	56.3%	66.8%
% Below 50%ile basic skills	20.0%	32.7%	24.9%
School Staffing			
Principal/Assistant Principal	4.0	4.0	4.0
Counselors	5.0	4.0	4.0
Librarians	1.5	2.0	2.0
Classroom and support teachers	70.0	72.0	77.0
Special education teachers	14.0	15.0	16.0
Service staff	38.5	41.5	47.5
Staff Attendance			
Principal/Assistant principal	100.0%	100.0%	100.0%
Counselors	99.2%	97.5%	98.2%
Librarians	97.1%	95.6%	94.6%
Classroom and support teachers	96.7%	95.6%	5.8%
Special education teachers	95.9%	95.0%	94.8%
Service staff	95.4%	95.7%	95.0%
ACT/SAT Testing Results			
Percent taking ACT	7.8%	69.9%	68.4%
ACT–English	19.3	20.1	20.4
ACT–Mathematics	18.7	19.5	18.3
ACT–Reading	20.2	21.1	21.3

TABLE 3.5 continued

ACT–Scientific Reasoning	20.4	21.1	20.6
ACT–Composite	19.8	20.6	20.3
% taking SAT	0.0%	24.5%	28.2%
SAT–Verbal	NA	451	443
SAT–Mathematics	NA	501	413
Honor Classes and Grades			
% Students in Honor classes	54.2%	52.1%	49.0%
Percent As	27.1%	26.8%	28.3%
Percent Bs	23.6%	23.7%	23.0%
Percent Cs	21.3%	22.7%	22.0%
Percent below C	24.0%	28.1%	28.6%
Other Performance Indicators			
Suspensions to Student Affairs	9	31	18
Drug and alcohol suspensions	24	20	9
Graduation rate	62.4	71.2	67.2
Drop-out Rate	16.1	12.9	24.5

Kanawha County Schools

establishing need. Additional data may be beneficial to include in a needs analysis process, such as a survey of remedial college classes high school graduates must take, or health department statistical summaries of physical and emotional needs of children in the community. A comprehensive need analysis is an ever-changing, on-going process that should be modified to meet current factors. Specific areas of concern may become apparent within a school or district during a school year. For example, a situation involving a violent act or racial tensions may occur that makes apparent a need that previously had not been considered. Items for consideration of need at the school and district level should be a local decision; however, a minimum consistent core listing of statistical data should be established.

Operations

The establishment of identified areas of need is critical in all aspects of school and system operation. Needs assessments should be developed for all functions of operation in the school system. The following are examples of defined areas of school system operation where factual information should be collected annually to determine level of efficiency and productivity:

- Personnel administration;
- Pupil transportation;
- Maintenance/energy management;
- Food service;
- Information systems;
- Communication;
- Finance/accounting; and
- Purchasing.

School districts should conduct an annual need assessment in all areas of operation. Data analyzed on a yearly basis should include information from at least the following areas: staff development evaluations, communications surveys, school effectiveness inventories, financial audit reports, food service audits, program reports, project evaluations, operation requests, accreditation reports, fire marshal reports, Board of Risk reports, maintenance summaries, and budget expenditure reports. In each operational area, defined state standards for performance and applicable minimum organizational standards, as well as best practice based on research findings, should be examined to establish what should be in place. Surveys, assessment instruments, and evaluation and audit reports should be utilized to assess current operational function and determine areas of need.

The following two examples provide recommendations for data that should be maintained, reviewed, and analyzed when determining need in operations area.

First, the maintenance area should maintain a tracking system to monitor number and type of maintenance requests completed, scheduled, or not accomplished in a given year. The tracking system should reflect the time required to schedule and complete each maintenance request. The tracking system should also reflect cost of materials, equipment, and labor and a satisfaction rating scale. A review of this data on maintenance requests enables department heads and planning teams to determine needs in terms of efficiency, personnel, and funding.

Second, the area of finance and accounting should maintain annual state audit reports that contain findings and recommendations that should be considered in a needs assessment process. School audit reports should be analyzed and lists of common findings of accounting violations should be noted for need determination purposes. Surveys should be taken to determine the finance department's efficiency and effectiveness in supporting school and other department concerns. Results of school and department surveys, audit reports, department employee recommendations/concerns, minimum organizational requirements, and known best practices based on research are important in determining need.

When developing a need assessment of operational area functions, establishment of a business advisory task force is generally recommended. The task force should consist of experts from major business and industry in the community with expertise in given operational areas. Experts from operational divisions within business and industry should conduct an assessment of the efficiency and effectiveness based on accepted best practices in non-educational settings. The assessment should establish a benchmark for what should exist. After the assessment is completed, a list of needs and recommendations for improvement should be developed.

Analysis of data in the operation area is the primary responsibility of the management team, supported by administrators in each department. Administrators should be responsible for involving staff and key constituent groups in determining data that needs to be maintained and analyzed in each operational area.

Facilities

State board policy or regulation usually guides the determination of facility needs. Most states require the development of comprehensive facility plans that reflect the facility needs of all schools within the district. The development of a comprehensive facility plan usually requires a review of at least the following categories of information:

1. Fire marshal reports—recommendations and citations.
2. Board of risk reports—recommendations and citations.
3. Asbestos management plans.
4. Energy conservation reports.
5. Prioritized maintenance lists.
6. Operation request analysis.
7. Enrollment reports.
8. Programmatic building requirement reports.
9. Facility cost/utilization reports.
10. Facility utilization reports.
11. Transportation schedules/timelines.

Each of these categories generates essential data for ascertaining comprehensive needs of a given building. It is important to consider all facets that affect the facility's effective utilization. Reviewing a list of maintenance needs is not sufficient to determine how effectively the facility meets the current curriculum requirements. A review of reports that outline program and course facility requirements should also be completed. An assessment of facility needs should include the following:

1. Current and projected maintenance requirements, including mandates from the fire marshal, Board of Risk and Management, asbestos survey reports, and energy utilization data;
2. Cost utilization reports that indicate energy efficiency and maximum space utilization;
3. Current and projected enrollment;
4. Current and anticipated programmatic requirements for space; and
5. Transportation times for current students and any projected redistricted students.

An analysis of all factors affecting facility needs is a basis for the development of reasonable and accurate facility improvement objectives that reflect actual need. Determining need is perhaps the least controversial part of the facility improvement process. The agreement by the community and school on how to address the needs (school consolidation, renovation, or closure), and then garnering support for funding the identified needs, are the major problems in the facility improvement process.

OBJECTIVE DEVELOPMENT

Objectives should be developed annually at each organizational level. School system objectives should reflect consideration of school and office objectives. Likewise, school and office objectives should reflect district system objectives.

System objectives, consisting of both focus and work objectives, should be understood, remembered, and clearly based on identified needs. Focus objectives need to be established with supporting work objectives. A limited number of focus objectives should address at least instruction, communication, finance, operations, and facilities. The focus objectives should be clearly communicated to all employees, LSICs, and the board. Each department and division should develop work objectives to support the focus objectives. It is each administrator's responsibility to communicate and support the focus objectives and to implement work objectives that accomplish the focus objectives.

This section provides a narrative description with pertinent information necessary for understanding each area for which objectives need to be developed: instruction, communication, finance, operation, and facilities. A listing of suggested focus and work objectives and anticipated results guide the development of district improvement plans. A narrative description for each area of improvement explains pre-requisite under-standings and requirements, or rationale for recommended system objectives.

Instruction

Narrative Description

Objectives for instructional improvement should raise student perform-ance on standardized test measures and have a positive impact on indica-tors that measure school effectiveness as it pertains to achievement, which include dropout rate, graduation rate, and grades. Specific areas of emphasis need to be addressed when developing objectives to improve student performance: (1) establishment of a solid academic foundation; (2) increased standards of performance; (3) provision for flexibility of time and program offerings; (4) enhancement of the arts; (5) increased staff development opportunities; (6) enhancement of technology in every aspect of the school system; and (7) increased accountability and moni-toring The following briefly explains the importance of each area.

Building a Solid Foundation. Objectives should be formulated that develop a structure that enhances opportunities for students to acquire fundamental reading skills. Success in reading is directly correlated with academic success. The establishment of a foundation that provides a structure to enhance each student's ability to acquire prerequisite reading skills is essential for improvement in the instructional area. Objectives should be formulated and implemented that establish a fundamental support structure in elementary schools that encompasses (1) enhanced services to families through a Family Resource Center to ensure that stu-dents come to school reading to learn; (2) increased opportunities for pre-school and Head Start educational services; (3) establishment of full-day kindergarten in all elementary schools; (4) reduction of class size in the primary grades; (5) avoidance of split grades in the primary unit; and (6) provision of one-on-one instruction to first-grade students who are not mastering pre-requisite reading skills.

Increased Standards. Raising standards and establishing higher expectations should be recurrent themes in the work objectives devel-oped to achieve the instructional focus or system objective. The following measures should be incorporated into instructional work objectives to achieve higher standards: (1) definition of required learning; (2) correla-tion of curriculum with standardized test measures; (3) increased gradu-ation requirements; (4) establishment of senior projects; (5) addition of required courses in speech, technology and career life skills; (6) establishment of minimum skill requirements; (7) establishment of instructional requirements such as science class instruction (must be 50 percent lab); (8) establishment of community service learning expectation; (9) placement of first-year college course requirements in all high schools; and (10) establishment of an international baccalaureate high school.

Flexibility of Time and Programs. Recognition of the importance of *time* on learning and the need to offer programs that are flexible and diverse is established in *Prisoners of Time*, the 1994 Report of the National Education Commission on Time and Learning. Educators recognize that everyone does not learn in the same way or in the same amount of time, but they do not always act on this in an aggressive committed fashion:

> With few exceptions,
> Schools open and close their doors at fixed times in the morning and
>   early afternoon.
> The school year lasts nine months.
> Schools typically offer a six-period day, 5.6 hours of classroom time.
> The schedule assigns an average of 51 minutes per class period.
>   (National Education Commission on Time and Learning 1994, 7)

Objectives should support the research found in the *Prisoners of Time* report. Initiatives that enhance the school system's ability to address diverse needs should be reflected in work objectives: (1) alternative evening high school programs that provide the opportunity to receive high school credits during evening hours; (2) on-line high school programs that provide structured completion of high school credits via the computer in students home and labs; (3) alternative junior/middle school for students whose behavior requires removal from the regular school setting; (4) extension of elementary school education for remediation and supplement to summer programs; (5) early graduation opportunities; (6) college credit in the public school setting; (7) summer high school for enrichment, not just remediation; and (8) use of block schedules.

Enhanced Arts Education Services. Research has confirmed what many have believed about music for over 700 years: music makes us smarter (Shaw, Rauscher, Levine, Wright, Newcomb 1997). Ensure that students develop this mark of an educated person—an appreciation and understanding of the arts—instructional work objectives should incorporate (1) art and music specialist services in all elementary schools; (2) restructuring of elementary music to focus on the Orff method of instruction; (3) establishment of a magnet elementary music school; (4) establishment of a county-wide elementary chorus; (5) establishment of a required fine arts credit for graduation; (6) establishment of partnerships with music associations and productions to provide direct support and instruction to students; and (7) establishment of alternative ways to earn credit through student participation in approved activities such as youth ballets and orchestras.

Staff Development. Commitment of resources to continue the learning process of all personnel is a necessary component for enhancing student and school system performance. Tony Alvarado, superintendent of School District #2 in New York City, where test scores increased from tenth to second in the city, addressed the 1997 Columbia University Superintendent Workshop. Alvarado concluded the only way to change student performance is to invest in professional development . . . "no other way to change students' performance than to change the knowledge and skills of those charged with delivering the instruction." While school systems' primary purpose is to educate all children, staff development of educators often is the subject of criticism.

Increased funding for staff development should stipulate that an amount of time be devoted to professional development, and staff development requirements should be included in all projects and plans of improvement. A five-year plan for comprehensive staff development needs should guide the development of necessary system and work objectives. Increased funds and time should be allocated to meet ongoing staff development. The work objectives should address initiatives that (1) commit additional funds to local schools to meet specific staff development requirements; (2) establish a process and program that enables each secondary school and elementary schools not meeting minimum performance requirements to receive whole school training; (3) requires staff development for school/office/system improvement plans; (4) offers structured staff development opportunities within the school calendar; and (5) establish leadership and teacher academies for teachers, principals, and aspiring administrators.

Technology. *Prisoners of Time* reinforces the need for school districts to expand and improve technology support and services. Objectives need to be developed to support technology initiatives that (1) expand Internet access in all schools; (2) provide area technology teachers to support effective implementation of instructional software; (3) expand support of technicians to address hardware issues; (4) redesign vocational technical classes to industrial technology labs in each junior high/middle school; (5) update business labs in all schools; and (6) develop a county-wide and school technology implementation/maintenance/replacement plan.

Accountability/Monitoring. The establishment and continued emphasis on an accountability system are essential to instructional improvement. Most effective is the knowledge of expectations coupled with a management system that determines the level of attainment. Objectives should support accountability initiatives throughout the school system: (1) establishment of required improvement plans and required management review procedures; (2) development of annual reports on school and school system progress; (3) development of a process for monitoring school improvement against minimum requirements; (4) establishment of a curriculum specialist position in each high school to monitor implementation of student minimum requirements and instructional standard requirements; (5) establishment of a process to gather data regarding high school graduates; (6) establishment of monitoring procedures for compliance with state and school accreditation standards; and (7) establishment of a student warranty certificate.

Instructional Focus Objective

All schools will meet or exceed state standards in the following indicators: graduation rate, drop-out rate, promotion/retention, state testing, school attendance, and school effectiveness.

Instructional Work Objectives

1. Develop individual school profiles reflecting relevant instructional student profile data each school year.
2. Develop individual school plans of improvement based upon relevant data each school year.
3. Develop and implement a process for regular and frequent monitoring of individual school plans of improvement.
4. Align curriculum with major concepts on state testing program.
5. Provide a five-day school-wide staff development for all secondary and elementary teachers on effective instructional strategies.
6. Require school progress reports/evaluation summaries on each school improvement plans.
7. Define; communicate to students, teachers, and parents; and monitor minimum course requirements in major subject areas in secondary schools.
8. Develop a career cluster program of studies.
9. Increase number and level of difficulty of course requirements for graduation.
10. Establish senior project requirement for graduation.
11. Establish student advisor program for all secondary students.

12. Expand accelerated reading programs in elementary and secondary schools.
13. Develop a consortium agreement with higher education to provide the first year of college courses in high schools (dual credit courses).
14. Establish full-day kindergarten in all elementary schools.
15. Expand preschool programs in all elementary schools.
16. Redesign Title I to provide instruction to first-level students experiencing difficulty with acquiring reading skills.
17. Redefine elementary music program to incorporate Orff instruction.
18. Provide art and music instruction by specialists to all elementary schools.
19. Establish an all-county elementary chorus.
20. Connect all schools to the Internet.
21. Employ technology specialists in each high school area.
22. Establish alternative evening high school programs
23. Develop an on-line home-based technology instructional program for alternative school students.
24. Establish a middle/junior high alternative school.
25. Establish a leadership staff development program for all prospective administrators.
26. Provide at least a minimum school-based level of funding at $10 per student for school based staff development programs.
27. Establish school-based funding for supplies, materials, and equipment at a minimum level of $100 per student.
28. Establish a character education program.
29. Establish family resource centers throughout the school system.
30. Employ curriculum supervisors for each high school.
31. Develop and receive special projects for instructional improvement in the amount of at least 1 percent of the operating budget.
32. Establish full-day faculty senates each month for staff development.
33. Establish a community service expectation for all secondary students.

Communications

Narrative Description

A comprehensive communication structure that supports all aspects of system operation and management is essential to school system success. The communication structure should be supported by appropriate focus and work objectives within the system improvement process. Superintendents and boards need to fully understand and commit to funding a comprehensive communication structure that includes two components: required administrative organization and communication vehicles to ensure on-going flow of information with constituent groups at all levels of operation.

Public education is a major business in most communities. Successful businesses effectively communicate and market efforts to increase community awareness of the quality of their product and business. School systems also need to effectively communicate and market their programs, services, and products, namely educated children. The United States is a consumer nation, and whose citizens often make decisions based on the marketing package presented. For example, the community believes "Coke is it" because that is the message that is marketed. The marketing package enables the business to attract the consumer to the product. The product then must be of sufficient quality for the consumer to continue to support it. School systems' communication strategies will let the community know and understand more about the education needs, requirements, programs, services, and successes. If communication is comprehensive and effective, public satisfaction with the school system may be demonstrated through increased parental and community participation and funding of levies and bonds.

An effective communication structure is expensive, and it requires an on-going financial commitment. However, it is important to understand that without effective communication structures, school systems face the prospect of diminished funding from all sources, such as federal and state grants, private sector awards, legislative allocations, and public approval of bonds and levies. The cost of funding a comprehensive communication structure is overridden by the community support it engenders for the school system, and the public's understanding of importance of funding public education at levels adequate to the meet the needs of today's students.

The components of an effective communication structure, administrative organization, and communication vehicles are part of an effective management system that should be supported by appropriate work objectives. Consideration of a school system's specific needs—in terms of size, community dynamics, and number and type of anticipated initiatives—determines the magnitude of communication support that needs to be in place.

The first component of an effective communication structure requires an adequate administrative organization that supports monitoring and implementing all communication vehicles and system objectives. The selection of a knowledgeable, articulate administrator to manage the communication department of a school system is important. The communication administrator needs to be experienced, demonstrate expertise in education and communication, and be a member of the management team and participate in assistant and associate team meetings. The communication administrator should be the primary person who works with the media and who stays current and knowledgeable about school system happenings. As such, it is important to advise the communication administrator of any developing issues or crisis in the school system.

This administrator should develop a comprehensive communication plan that includes media activities and communication vehicles. Sufficient public relation support staff needs to be in place to accomplish the labor-intensive activities associated with communication efforts. (If a school system's size restricts the allocation of sufficient communication staff, then districts should consider sharing a communication department/structure.) Support staff should include public relation coordinator(s), television director for school district(s) television channel, film crew, graphic artist(s), photographers, journalists, secretaries, and clerks. The level of investment in sufficient expert staff parallels the success of implementing comprehensive media activities and communication vehicles.

The second component of an effective communication structure are communication vehicles enable all constituent groups at every operational level to send and receive information. Presence of sufficient communication vehicles that should be determined by an application of the Communication Synergy Cycle model. An effective communication structure within a school district requires the application of the communication synergy model to define communication gaps that need to be filled. Communication vehicles include media (television, radio, and newspaper), publications, visitations, independent studies, performance assessments, staff development, accreditation process, surveys, meetings, school system television channels, system objectives, plans of improvement, citizen complaints, policies, advisory committees, forums, dialogues, and conferences. These should be vehicles to acquire and send information from each constituent group: community (parents, business, industry, government, and senior citizens), the board, management team, school and office personnel, and students.

The communication department should monitor the presence and use of adequate communication vehicles. Sufficient communication vehicles provide on-going opportunities necessary to educate all constituent groups about the school system operation, management system, and improvement process. An understanding of school system operation, garnered through a variety of opportunities to participate, yields communities that support school system needs.

Communication Focus Objective

To improve communications by fostering public trust, encourage involvement and create support so that students, parents, school system employees, and the community will be informed, interested, and actively involved in public education within the school system.

Communication Work Objectives

1. Establish an administrative structure that includes a communication director and necessary support staff.
2. Develop a comprehensive communication plan that defines media activities and communication vehicles.
3. Develop necessary communication vehicles where gaps exist as determined by application of communication synergy model.
4. Establish forums/dialogues with students and staff for discussing cultural diversity/multicultural issues.
5. Establish student dialogues at each high school with superintendent and administrative staff, principal, and faculty senate chair.
6. Establish informational conferences for students, staff, and community on higher standards, cultural diversity, and safe schools.
7. Establish a superintendent advisory committee composed of representatives from all employee groups within the system.
8. Establish an advisory committee for communications consisting of public relation and media experts.
9. Establish dialogues with board and communities on facility needs/concerns and funding.
10. Establish monthly meetings between superintendent and teacher and principal organizations.
11. Establish an employee publication.
12. Establish a student publication.
13. Establish weekly communication reports to the board.
14. Require a communication component for each school/department plan of improvement.
15. Develop and distribute an annual report on school system accomplishments.
16. Establish an academic scholars foundation that distributes $1,000 annually to each honor graduate.
17. Develop a recognition process for student and employee accomplishments.

18. Develop a comprehensive programming schedule for the television channel that focuses on individual school and school district initiatives and accomplishments.
19. Implement a minority recruitment program.
20. Schedule regular meetings between the superintendent and management team with outside organizations, such as chamber of commerce, business and industry development corporations, higher education councils, and so on.
21. Administer a system wide and community survey requesting input on all areas of school system operation—instruction, communication, finance, operation, and facilities.
22. Secure input on all new policies and proposed changes in existing policies.
23. Establish a comprehensive communication task force to determine effectiveness of communication strategies.
24. Develop and distribute brochures on the school system, special projects, and initiatives.
25. Provide weekly press releases summarizing events, activities, and programs of interest within the school system.
26. Distribute informational press releases on topics of special interest at least every ten days.

Finance

Narrative Description

To achieve fiscal responsibility and a balanced budget for a school system in an era when nonrestricted funds, are declining, state and federal mandates are increasing and funding that is based primarily on student enrollment is virtually impossible. Before listing the focus and work objectives to be considered for implementation to improve fiscal management, it is important to understand the funding mechanism, imposed budget restrictions, and requirements necessary for good fiscal management.

Funding Mechanisms. Most school districts' general operating budget is garnered from two sources: state and local revenues. The percent of state and local funding varies with each state. Most school districts receive the majority of their revenue through local funds raised by the application of regular levy rates to assessed property values. However, some districts are more dependent on state funding formulas; they receive almost 65 percent of funds from state dollars and 35 percent from local funds. The allocation of state funds is usually contingent on student enrollment, with special consideration of additional funding for exception children. The greatest cost to school districts is salaries. Most school districts spend over 85 percent of their revenue on personnel salaries and related costs. Approximately 10 percent of a school system's budget is usually categorized as "current expense" and allows little opportunity for discretionary spending. After required expenses for payment of disposal, insurance for facilities and risk management, utilities, and repair and maintenance, only a minimal amount of funds remain for allocation to supplies, equipment, travel, and contractual agreements. The funding requests for "current expense" usually exceed funding capacity.

Imposed Budget Restrictions. Complicating school system fiscal management is the continuing number of unfunded federal and state mandates and court orders. Table 3.6 is a list of the unfunded mandates in a single year within Kanawha County Schools, most of which continuously affect a school system's operating budget.

TABLE 3.6 Unfunded Mandates FY 1994–95

Program	Effect FY 1994–95	Estimated Total Program Effect
Full-day kindergarten	1,338,000	$3,679,000
WVEIS	356,560	500,000
PEIA–local share	348,376	continuous
Pupil-teacher ratio—local share	220,000	continuous
Public Libraries from regular levy	1,562,490	continuous
Basic skills—computers—Jostens	80,000	800,000
Underfunding in state aid formula:		
Worker's Compensation at .99%	179,000	continuous
Risk & Management Insurance	108,000	continuous
Fire code changes	50,000	$5,000,000
Refuse removal	50,000	continuous
Reduced teacher/pupil ratio	359,586	$1,164,622
Service personnel shift differential	9,000	continuous
Planning periods	undetermined	continuous
Extended school year	undetermined	continuous
Federal chiller replacement	215,000	$1,500,000
Federal ADA disability	250,000	3,000,000
Federal asbestos	50,000	1,000,000
Federal gas tank, blood tests	30,000	continuous

Kanawha County Schools

New legislation without sufficient funding, a major problem for school systems, may devastate an already restricted budget. Unfunded mandates negatively impact a school system's financial stability during the year of implementation, but also may sustain on-going damage to the operating budget of a school system. But while legislative and congressional mandates may hurt the budget, they may bring about improvement in various aspects of system operation, instruction, or facilities. Planning for existing or anticipated unfunded mandates is an important part of good fiscal management. It is also prudent to build a level of discretionary funding within the budget in deference to unknown mandates that may occur during a school year. Management teams, administrators, and teacher organizations need to advocate for laws that limit or eliminate unfunded mandates. Effective communication strategies, including meetings with members of the legislature and government officials, should enhance awareness of the negative financial ramifications of unfunded mandates.

Effective Fiscal Management Requirements. Perhaps the most important component of effective fiscal management in a school system is the selection of knowledgeable treasurer. Fiscal improvement may not take place without a knowledgeable, skilled treasurer. The difficult task of finding an individual with the necessary skills is complicated by salary issues. Individuals with the skills necessary to effectively serve as treasurer for a $250 million school system budget are usually able to earn significantly more than most school systems provide, in another job—where they are exempt from attending a multitude of board meetings. Quality guidance from the school system's treasurer is essential to fiscal management and to any initiatives for improvement. Included in Harry Reustle's *Seven Habits of a Highly Effective Financial Superintendent* are crucial recommendations that should serve to guide administrative actions and the development of system objectives (Reustle 1996).

Seven Habits of Highly Effective Financial Superintendents

1. Define role and select your treasurer with care.
2. Know thy budget process well.
3. Understand the formula conflict.
4. Budget at net property taxes.
5. Understand and apply the "D" scale.
6. Allocate a surplus with wisdom.
7. Avoid cost avoidance. (Reustle)

Reustle' s financial advisory principles provide instruction and support on critical budgetary issues and help determine system and work objectives that should improve fiscal accountability. The principles should be used as a training tool for board members and system administrators. Reustle's definitions and explanations of habits of financially effective superintendents, excerpted below, are applicable in all school districts and need to be utilized as an important reference source for superintendents and boards.

Define Role and Select Your Treasurer With Care

The treasurer's position on the organization chart should be equal to the highest ranked and paid curriculum position. The treasurer should report directly to the superintendent and to no one else.

The treasurer should meet these characteristics:

1. The treasurer should be highly competent and highly ethical.
2. The treasurer should be a CPA (Certified Public Account). Do not select an educator. For your survival, you need a highly trained accountant that can respond to problems not covered in a textbook. The accountant should be skilled and knowledgeable in the business environment. Your image before the business community will depend upon your treasurer's financial counsel.
3. You should select an individual that professes and practices high standards of integrity, loyalty, and discipline with an aversion to power. The individual must have the objectivity to tell you, "No!" Since the treasurer has more finance technical knowledge than you, you must listen to the treasurer carefully and you *must* question the treasurer until you understand what the treasurer is saying to you. If you are politically centered or autocratic, you will fail.

Know Thy Budget Process Well

1. If you are unable to answer the public's question on how the school system is funded, the public will think you are deceiving them and you will fail.
2. Understanding the budget should be at the top of your priority list. The budget is the foundation for all the curriculum ideas you want done.
3. You must understand the significance of staffing ratios as it relates available revenues. A board of education is labor intensive and salaries with taxes will consume 85% of the budget. An error in matching your staffing to the state and local revenues will create a deficit.

Budget at Net Property Taxes

Property taxes are calculated from the market values and assessed values of properties within a county. The assessed values of properties are multiplied by the levy tax rates of different property classes. The product is a gross property tax amount. From the gross amount, a percentage is subtracted in order to provide for uncollectible tax delinquencies and forfeitures. After the amount for uncollectible tax delinquencies and forfeitures are subtracted from the gross, the resultant amount is a net property tax amount.

Budgeting levy taxes at net will generate additional revenues next fiscal year if tax delinquencies and forfeitures are low. These additional revenues are needed to cover unfunded state mandated requirements for the next fiscal year. You are in an inflexible financial environment. You can not lay off teachers in the middle of the year as a business would if the business were in financial trouble. If you budget your expenditures near the gross property tax amount, your school system will go deficit.

Understand and Apply the D Scale

The D scale (deficit scale) is a long-term graphical tool to predict if a school system is going deficit.

If you can predict with reasonable accuracy ahead of time that your school system is developing financial stress, you can better protect yourself and your school system. If you ignore, the trend of the D scale, you will fail.

The school system must maintain a level net cash from operations or an increasing net cash from operations to keep the system from going deficit.

Net cash from operations is the excess of general budget revenues over general budget expenditures. This concept is similar to "net income from operations" in the business world. A school district's annual financial statement includes restricted revenues and expenses from federal, state, and local grants.

Be fiscally conservative with current expenditures. Watch the trend on the D scale. If you do not watch the trend on the D scale, your school system will be going deficit without really knowing it.

Allocate a Surplus With Wisdom

A surplus is the excess of unencumbered general budget cash over general budget expenditures at June 30th.

If you do not allocate a surplus wisely, you will increase the rate at which your school system will go deficit. If your school system goes deficit, you will be criticized for poor fiscal management and you will fail.

1. Always allocate a surplus to salaries, taxes, and fringe benefits first. The amount of the surplus allocation to salaries, taxes, and fringes should be at least equal to the prior fiscal year's June 30, excess of salaries, taxes, and fringes over the original salaries, taxes, and fringes budget. This prior fiscal year's June

30, excess of salaries, taxes, and fringes over their original budgets, is due to paying unfunded state mandated pupil/ teacher ratio position requirements.

2. Always allocate the surplus next to any known deficient budget accounts that you forecast will be insufficient to cover that budget account's expenses.

3. Allocate the remaining surplus to board and administration desires.

4. Never first allocate a surplus to board member *desires*. Protect them. Allocate a surplus to their desires last.

Avoid Cost Avoidance

Cost avoidance is a non-accounting term representing estimated unrestricted general budget expenditures avoided due to consolidation. The term is a heating and cooling term.

The cost avoidance concept assumes that all costs will remain constant in the future. However, in practice, costs increase because of inflation, federal and state mandates, and board priorities. Thus, the cost efficiency involved with cost avoidance is consumed by other cost increases. The budget will increase in spite of cost avoidance measures.

Positions that will be reduced from consolidation of schools will have a cost avoidance effect on salaries for one year. After that one year, the state funding formula will adjust to the reduction in positions. Thus, the benefit from cost avoidance on reduced salary expenditures is for one year only, not several years.

Cost avoidance from consolidations will have an effect on repairs and maintenance, transportation, and utilities for a period greater than one year. However, the caution mentioned in one above is applicable and the cost avoidance benefit becomes less as years pass on.

(Reustle 1996)

Finance Focus Objective

To develop and maintain a balance budget that supports the educational needs of the students.

Finance Work Objectives

1. Fund service and professional positions at 100 percent level of known costs.

2. Develop a budget based on estimated revenues to be received from net property taxes.

3. Establish a program to reduce substitute cost by allocating funds to schools with unused substitute monies at the end of fiscal year.
4. Establish and maintain a separate long-term substitute account.
5. Establish and maintain a permanent improvement account of at least 2 percent of the total operating budget.
6. Build a permanent improvement account balance of more than 2 percent of the operating budget to address specific facility improvement projects.
7. Maintain an A1 bond rating in order to receive lowest interest rate when bonds are issued for facility construction.
8. Establish a carry-over balance sufficient to cover necessary unfunded expenditures that were excluded from the preliminary budget.
9. Sell all surplus property.
10. Provide salary increases to all employees on a regular basis.
11. Maintain an excess levy (in applicable states) to meet financial needs of the school system.
12. Maintain a regular levy rate at a level necessary to address known need expenditures.
13. Receive approval for bond issues for funding of comprehensive facility improvement plans.
14. Establish an indirect cost rate sufficient to meet local expenses for project management.
15. Correlate budget priorities with the system improvement process.

Operations

Narrative Description

A major responsibility of a school system is the provision of an array of business support and auxiliary services that address the daily operational aspects of the school system, including personnel, pupil transportation, maintenance, purchasing, food service, purchasing, and information systems. The efficiency of these areas of operation is important to keeping "the train on the track." Unfortunately, funds for operation areas are usually insufficient. (Personnel department is an exception because in school districts, funding for salaries constitutes the majority of the budget.) Maintenance in many school systems is funded at 50 percent of identified need. Opportunities for "laying new track" are restricted by funding availability. School system operations need to be managed by an individual who is educated and experienced in business management. The operational aspect of a school system is increasingly more complex, with funds more limited and demands greater, which usually results in less successful management of operations for a school district.

The selection of a qualified business manager with demonstrated experience and education in business or industry is essential for improving efficiency within operation functions. It is all too common for school systems to select principals and coaches with demonstrated ability to run a small business and/or make money outside the school system as the chief administrator for operations. Unfortunately, the complexities of managing large maintenance crews, understanding energy conservation measures and air quality issues, and establishing purchasing practices and inventory controls are not part of an education administrator's certificate program.

The structure of operation areas in terms of work assignments is important. In a management system that supports site-based decision-making, the structure of operations needs to reflect local involvement and support. The maintenance department should be assigned in attendance areas in order to enhance involvement in local school improvement and to establish a higher level of accountability. In large school systems, maintenance workers should be assigned in teams to serve a specific group(s) of schools. In all areas within the operation division, ties or associations with specific schools need to be established. Operation workers need to be part of school(s) support team. Employees need to be part of a team not only within their field of expertise, such as electrical, painting, transportation, or information systems, but also within a school(s). This team-building with schools ensures that everyone shares in the success of the schools and also feels a commitment to addressing school problems and concerns.

Since most of the operations responsibilities are outside school systems' core level of expertise—instruction—it is important that educators establish a network of business and industrial experts who serve as advisors. These experts, whether they serve as part of a business advisory task force and or an advisory committee for a specific department, should assist in determining needs, developing objectives for improvement, and evaluating results. All offices within the operation department should establish a standing advisory committee of outside experts and employee representatives to identify concerns and make recommendations for solving problems and bringing about improvement.

In a school system, it is important to remember that operation is a service-support function that enables the system to achieve its core purpose of educating children.

The efficiency of each operation area has enormous impact on school system success:

1. *Personnel:* How well you select, hire, support in benefits and adhere to personnel laws and policies;
2. *Transportation:* How well you transport students to and from school in terms of safety and time in transport;
3. *Maintenance/Energy Management:* how well you maintain clean, attractive, energy-efficient buildings;
4. *Food Service:* how well you provide good, wholesome, and appealing food that children enjoy;
5. *Information System:* how well you support the use and maintenance of technology software and equipment in administration offices and classrooms; and
6. *Purchasing:* how well you define practices, procedures, and policies to guide all purchasing that acquires the highest quality products at the lowest cost for schools and offices.

Operation Focus Objective

To improve the productivity, level of service, and cost-efficiency for maintenance, energy management, custodial support, facilities planning, purchasing, food services, information systems, transportation, personnel, and emergency response/safety/security as measured by implementation of business advisory committee recommendations and cost analysis/productivity reports.

Operation Work Objectives

1. Establish a business advisory committee to review all present operations and to provide recommendations for improving efficiency and decreasing cost.
2. Implement recommendations made by the business advisory committee.
3. Establish an advisory committee for each operational function area.
4. Employ a business manager with education and experience in business and industry operations and management.
5. Employ adequate number of supervisors for every operational area to provide for optimum monitoring and accountability.
6. Centralize all purchasing of food service.
7. Establish direct billing system for all student meals.

8. Establish a quality food service student advisory committee that recommends menus.
9. Assign maintenance and transportation workers to specific school(s) support teams.
10. Utilize software that tracks number and type of operation requests for each school.
11. Establish flexible and straight timeshifts for all maintenance workers.
12. Require direct reporting to work of all maintenance workers.
13. Establish a school cleanliness monitoring process.
14. Establish a schedule to paint all schools every five years.
15. Establish an employee recruitment plan that secures adequate number of new teachers to meet program demand and retirements.
16. Institute a professional computerized substitute call-out system.
17. Establish a monitoring system to ensure completion of all service and professional evaluations.
18. Implement a work-site wellness program.
19. Implement an absentee reduction plan.
20. Establish commodity-buying councils.
21. Reduce surplus furniture and equipment inventories.
22. Reduce commodity inventories by increasing direct shipments to schools.
23. Implement a computerized system for developing transportation schedules and generating redistricting options.
24. Reduce the number of bus terminals.
25. Install video cameras in all school buses.
26. Establish bus schedules to ensure no student spends more that forty-five minutes one way on the bus.
27. Establish emergency response procedures/plan.

Facilities

Narrative Description

Addressing facility needs in a school system is a complicating, frustrating endeavor. The sources of funding to support major facility repair, renovation, and new construction are limited. In most states, three primary sources support facility renovation and construction, specific state allocations of funds for facilities; bonds; and local school district's capital or permanent improvement fund. Each of these avenues of funding are important to understand prior to developing system objectives for facilities. Each source has specific restrictions and limitations that affect availability of revenue to support needed facility projects. A brief description of each source is reviewed.

State Funds. In most states, special legislation establishes a certain level of funding to support new construction and major renovations. School districts are required to submit projects to the state funding agency for new construction or major renovation of facilities. Applications for state funds are usually submitted on an annual basis, and dollars are appropriated within the agency's funding capacity. The limited amount of funding restricts the dollars available to distribute to school districts. Most requests for funds for new construction must demonstrate a high level of commitment of local funds, either through the school system's permanent improvement fund or an approved bond issue. The application process is highly competitive. In many states the facility application must demonstrate that new construction results in school closures and that local funds, such as bonds or capital improvement dollars, are available to match state funds. Usually the level of funding is inadequate to meet school facility needs throughout the state. In addition, most states establish funding mechanisms to address emergency facility issues, such as schools destroyed by fire or natural disaster.

Bonds. The second avenue for funding facility construction and renovation is a bond initiative. Bonds require voter approval. In an era of tax revolt, it is difficult to receive support of the citizens. Comprehensive bond issues are problematic for a number of reasons: Bonds raise taxes, and bonds generally result in consolidation of buildings.

The level of planning and necessary involvement of community, school, administration, and board are enormous in preparation for a bond. Justification for a bond is usually included within the school district's comprehensive facility plan. When developing a comprehensive facility plan for a school district, the funds required to address facility renovation and construction should be pinpointed. Included within the plan should be recommendations to request funds from specific sources: bonds, permanent improvement accounts, and state authority. Major facility projects require funding that exceeds most school system's general operating budget. The process for development of a school district's comprehensive facility plan generates much controversy. The process must include opportunity for school, faculty, parents, and community representatives to discuss their needs and define their expectations. Generally each school expects a state-of-the-art facility in their own community, with school closures designated somewhere else. School closures are only necessary if it is not "your" school.

The process for developing a comprehensive facility plan may prompt the departure of the superintendent. There is a tendency to place blame if "your" community school is the one slated for closure, or if redistricting aligns a disproportionate number of low-income students, or if renovation rather than new construction recommended in the facility plan.

Capital Improvement Funds. Most state statutes provide school districts with the authority to establish a capital improvement fund. The establishment of this fund should be a priority budget consideration for a school district. Enormous financial commitments restrict the school system's ability to fund a capital improvement account at any significant level. However, a capital improvement account is essential for dealing with facility emergencies: broken heating systems; collapsed roofs; and buildings damaged by floods, fires, and storms. School districts should strive to maintain at least 2 percent of their average operating budget in a capital improvement account. When the amount for capital improvement exceeds the 2 percent level, funds may be used to support permanent improvement projects. A school district's demonstrated ability to fund a capital improvement account is advantageous in seeking approval of bond or state funds. Local school district commitment to fund a capital improvement account demonstrates good fiscal management.

Facility Focus Objective

To provide the best possible facilities that meet health and safety standards and the educational needs of the students, staff, and community in the most economical manner.

Facility Work Objectives

1. Increase funds to address fire code violations in order to achieve full compliance with fire marshal recommendations.
2. Develop a comprehensive education facility plan for the school district.
3. Develop a facility improvement project and secure funding from state funding authority.
4. Develop and offer a comprehensive bond to secure funds for needed renovation and construction delineated in the facility plan.
5. Develop and implement two- to five-year plans for painting, paving, America With Disabilities Act (ADA) compliance, fire code compliance, and HVAC requirements within each school.
6. Develop and implement a weekly review of school maintenance issues.

7. Design and implement an energy management plan.
8. Maintain a capital improvement fund of at least 2 percent of the average operational budget.
9. Assign dollars within the capital improvement fund in excess of 2 percent of total operating budget to specific major school renovation or new construction projects.

Accountability/Results

Monitoring

Monitoring progress toward meeting system objectives (focus and work) requires an effective management system that provides for a limited span of control, prescribed assessment instruments, and comprehensive annual progress reports. Comprehensive objectives should be evaluated annually for degree and level of progress, completion, and implementation. Department heads and area assistant superintendents should generate quarterly and annual progress reports. All management team meetings need to allocate time to review progress and address concerns relating to system objectives.

Employee professional development plans should relate to the progress that needs to be made in specific objective improvement areas. Superintendent and management team personnel evaluations should also be based on a determination of system objective progress.

Annual reports should reflect progress made in implementing system objectives. At retreats, management team members and principals should review need and analyze progress. School-wide training should reflect schools' improvement plans, evaluation components, and progress.

A direct correlation exists between the level and amount of planning, monitoring and accountability, and system progress. Education has often depended on the ability of any one given administrator to ensure an effective school or school system. The management system described in preceding chapters lessens the need for individual "educational heroes" by increasing all performance expectations, monitoring more frequently, and intervening appropriately when needed. A management system that requires frequent monitoring and implementation of prescribed curricular requirements and state standards, increases the ability of every individual in the system to improve efficiency and effectiveness. A management system that holds each individual responsible for specific and measurable objectives and requirements increases the likelihood of improved operation and educational progress. Table 3.7 lists the various accountability and monitoring measures that may be utilized in an effective management system.

TABLE 3.7 Accountability and Monitoring Measures

1.	School improvement plans/school objectives/evaluation
2.	County improvement plans/system objectives/evaluation
3.	School accreditation process mandated by state
4.	County accreditation process mandated by state
5.	Annual report of system progress
6.	Site-based administration—area assistant superintendents and area support teams
7.	School intervention process
8.	School report card
9.	County report card
10.	School profile report
11.	Audit reports
12.	Fire marshal reports
13.	Board of Risk reports
14.	Operation request tracking system
15.	Surveys
16.	School Effectiveness Inventory
17.	State/county student testing program
18.	Employee and management team evaluation system
19.	Transportation safety reports
20.	Project evaluation reports
21.	Awards and recognitions

Results/Progress

Developing a comprehensive plan for school and school system improvement requires a foundation of essential elements for success: analysis of statistical and factual data to determine needs; annual development of objectives at each organizational level; design and implementation of an accountability system that holds all participants, students, teachers, service personnel, and administration to a high standard of performance; and, completion of an annual report of progress/results. The system improvement process should result in defined, verifiable accomplishments, with progress made in all major facets of the school system. Definition of what should be accomplished in each of the areas of focus with the implementation of an effective improvement process and management system is important. The definition of outcomes motivates those who have supported the establishment of a minimum organizational requirements, management system, and improvement process to remain involved and committed to continued implementation at every operational level. The anticipated outcomes assist in monitoring system progress. The following list of anticipated system outcomes is based on the previously defined focus and work objectives.

Instruction Results

- Standardized test scores increase in grades K–12.
- Number of schools on state academic probation reduced.
- Dropout rate reduced.
- Attendance improved.
- Grades improved.
- SAT verbal and math scores increased.
- Graduation statistics improved:
  - Percent attending college;
  - Percent employed;
  - Percent in the military;
  - Percent in vocational school; and
  - Percent unemployed.
- Number of students completing college courses in high school increased.
- Number of students completing Advanced Placement (AP) courses increased.
- Number of students completing international baccalaureate program increased.

Communication Results

- Opportunities for students, employees, the board and the community to receive and send information regarding the school system exist in all defined vehicles as illustrated by the synergy cycle.
- All high school students complete a community service project each year.
- School effectiveness inventories improve in public, staff and students positive perception of school and school system.
- Community surveys show improved satisfaction rate with school system.
- Number of positive newspaper articles and radio and television shows increase on an annual basis.
- Number of grievances and citizen complaints reduced.
- Excess and regular levies approved by the community at levels sufficient to meet financial needs of the school system.

- Bonds approved by the community to meet facility needs.

Finance Results

- Balanced budget maintained.
- Bond rating maintained at A1 level.
- Amount of surplus property reduced.
- Annual substitute costs decrease.
- Carry-over balance addressed unfunded budget requests.
- Salary increases provided for all employees on a regular basis.
- Capital improvement monies exist for emergencies and facilities improvement projects.
- Dollars increased at the local level for supplies, equipment, travel, staff development.
- Funds provided through bonds and state authority for facility improvement/construction projects.
- Regular and excess levy rates approved at levels sufficient to meet school system needs.

Operations Results

- Cost savings increased and services improved in all operational areas, including maintenance, energy management, facilities, purchasing, food service, transportation, personnel, and information systems through increased efficiency as measured by survey.
- Schools clean and attractive, and operation requests completed in a timely manner.
- Participation increased and satisfaction rate improved with food service as measured by a student survey.
- Satisfaction rating on school effectiveness inventory as it relates to building up-keep increased.

Facility Improvement Results

- Fire code violations addressed in a timely manner.
- Board of Risk citations and findings addressed.
- Funds secured through local capital improvement funds, state authorization, and bond(s) to address facility needs identified in the comprehensive facility plan.

- Increased cost savings as a result of implementation of energy conservation measures.

SUMMARY

A clearly defined system improvement process that is understood and supported by boards, superintendent, administrators, teachers, and service personnel is essential for "laying new track." This process is a long-term continuous effort to bring positive results and progress.

The system improvement process presented in this chapter includes specific components: an agreed-upon foundation that establishes what is essential and/or important for effective schools; a needs assessment process that identifies deficiencies at each operational level that should be addressed; an objective development process that delineates broad-based focus objectives and specific work objectives that are measurable; and an accountability commitment that regularly assesses the results or level of progress in attaining objectives. The system improvement process requires involvement and implementation at each level of operation. Schools, departments, and offices should develop improvement plans that identify need, establish objectives, and provide a method of evaluating results. The county-wide improvement (education) plan should be based on input from every constituency group, including community, schools, central office personnel, and the board. The system objectives generated should reflect an understanding of needs at the local level as defined in their school/department improvement plans. Likewise, individual school objectives should be designed to support the system objectives. Plans of improvement at each level of operation should be interconnected with the system objectives.

A system improvement process establishes a common direction or focus for the school system. System objectives, which define and address common areas of need, should be clearly understood and supported by staff efforts at every level of operation. Without an effective system improvement process, the complexities of operating a school system may prevent establishment of common direction of efforts for progress.

Improvement of a school system is a continuous, never-ending process. The end is never reached, and the improvement process should provide for sustaining the system while renewal and development occurs. This sustaining, renewal and development must include everyone in the process: teachers, service personnel, administrators, board members, parents, students, community members, government officials, and business and industry representatives—or at least everyone must have confidence in the system and where the system is going in order not to become a detractor or interloper in the process. (Young 1995, 1)

Establishing the core components of minimum organizational requirements, a management system, and an improvement process are imperative for making school systems work—for "keeping the train on the track, laying new track, and keeping peace in the valley." In addition, an understanding of the complexities of school system operation is a prerequisite for establishing the core components that make school systems work. Chapter 4, detailing the complexities of school system operation, is constructed to provide readers with tangible examples of major issues, tasks, and crises that must be addressed daily to keep the school system operating.

System Operation: "Keeping the Train on the Track"

Organizations are more appropriately characterized as organic
... living, growing systems in which various units contribute to
the vitality in complex ways, not in simple, mechanical fashion.

—JERRY PATTERSON, *COMING CLEAN*
ABOUT ORGANIZATIONAL CHANGE

INTRODUCTION

School system operation is a major endeavor for a management system. Management systems should strive to maintain effective system operation that "keeps the train on the track and peace in the valley," and implement comprehensive system improvement that "lays new track." The two major functions of school system management, operation and improvement, are interconnected. However, operation is often the only endeavor that a management system may be able to address. The demands of school system operation or "keeping the train on the track and peace in the valley" may prevent or greatly hinder management from addressing school system improvement, or "laying new track."

Understanding school system operation is important to those who expect system improvement. School system operation may be divided into three categories or concerns: (1) major issues; (2) major routine tasks; and (3) daily crises. A management system should provide for effectively and efficiently addressing each operational category as well as administering system improvement initiatives or objectives. Items within each category of system operation may divert focus away from accomplishing objectives/initiatives that move the system forward. A management system with clear principles, priorities, and objectives guides administrator's decisions and actions when addressing tasks, issues, and crises.

Response to the operational category concerns may be fragmented and disjointed without a clear understanding of what is to be achieved; namely, a common management focus. Addressing operational issues, tasks, and crises is time-consuming and labor-intensive. An effective management system with a clear vision and objectives is essential for successfully addressing all operational categories.

Developing a comprehensive understanding of school system operation is important for staff, board members, and interested community members. Understanding the complexity of system operation better enables constituents to "keep the train on the track." Community members, board members, legislators, state administrators, media, senior citizens, and school employees who judge the performance of an educational system need to understand the composition of each operational category: the daily issues, tasks, and crises. Ability to address each area of concern is an accomplishment in and of itself. Moving the system forward based on agreed-upon system objectives is a "bonus," and those who judge educational systems should understand this. The larger the school district, the greater the chance for misunderstandings to develop in each area of concern. Some observers might conclude that size may negatively impact system improvement. (Schlechty 1997, 77).

The remaining sections of this chapter review each operational category and provide relevant situations that serve as examples of issues, tasks, and crises.

MAJOR SYSTEM ISSUES

Major issues are often imposed upon the system from an outside source, such as the state legislature, state government, federal mandate, election results, court order, concerned citizen(s), and community groups. Major issues may also emanate from staff action or inaction or may be board-generated. A major issue requires attention over an extended period, and its key characteristics are conflict and unrest. The major issues discussed in this section are not necessarily localized but are applicable in school systems throughout the country. Major issues are most frequently related to school system funding or budget problems but may also generate from social, political, or administrative decisions that upset a segment of any constituency group.

State Reduction in Funds

Any significant reduction in funding to a local education agency may become a major issue for a school system. The amount and timing of fund reduction determines the magnitude of the financial issue the school system must address. If the funding reduction occurs after the budget is developed and approved based on anticipated revenue, the ramifications may be greater than if reduction occurs before the budget is finalized.

Reduction of funds may occur for a variety of reasons. In most school districts, revenue is at least partially based on property taxes. If a major corporation bankrupts, relocates, or is destroyed, large revenues for a school district may be lost. The state also allocates school district funding. If the state recommends a funding reduction, the school system may suffer a major loss of revenue. These reductions may become a major issue for a school district.

How a school district addresses the reduction in funds may be complicated by necessary legal action. When a large company bankrupts, litigation by the school district may be necessary to receive some preference for revenue in the disposition of the company's assets. A school district may also find it necessary to bring litigation against the state to determine if school districts should be given immunity in funding reductions as compared with other state agencies. The reduction in funds may result in insufficient revenue to cover expenses and a deficit situation may occur. The school district may need to eliminate any vacant positions in order to reduce the number of personnel and corresponding cost. Reduction in personnel negatively affects programs and services and heightens staff and community concern. Administration action may also require that all currently funded items in the budget be re-evaluated for possible elimination. Subsequent reduction in funds for substitutes, supplies, materials, equipment, non-essential maintenance projects, staff development, extracurricular activities, and contract services may increase dissatisfaction and unrest throughout the school system and community. Once individuals are given approval for a position, project, or service, they react negatively when authorization is revoked.

The Failure of an Excess Levy or Reduction in Regular Levy Rate

Most school districts receive the majority of their funding through the application of a regular levy rate to assessed property values. In states dependent on the levy rate, there are usually few restrictions on the establishment of the rate. However, if the rate is substantially lowered, school systems may have insufficient revenue to meet the previously funded staff, equipment, supplies, and so on. Faced with a decline in revenue from the regular levy, a school district must implement strategies to reduce cost throughout the school system.

A few states have provided authorization for school systems to seek approval from the public for excess levies to support school system operation. The excess levy is in addition to the regular levy rate applied to property values. Excess levies, based on application of additional tax rate on property values, are approved by the voters for a specific duration and must be voted on again before the expiration date for continuation. The loss of an excess levy in an election negatively affects a school system. The designated use and the amount of revenue secured from the excess levy determine the level of impact of a failed levy. A failed excess levy diverts the superintendent's and administration's attention to word establishing: (1) processes for securing a new election for reconsideration and approval of an excess levy; and (2) steps that need to be immediately instituted to reduce current expenditures.

The failure of an excess levy or the reduction of the regular levy rate is a major issue because it requires attention over an extended period of time, and conflict and unrest is associated with the steps that may be instituted to reduce present and future expenditures. When an excess levy fails or the regular levy rate is reduced, the funding loss occurs in the next fiscal year. However, the amount of anticipated revenue loss requires the administration to begin immediately restricting and eliminating current anticipated expenditures. The immediate restriction makes available funds to support essential items within the next fiscal year. Spending reductions might include limiting purchase of supplies, materials, and equipment; reducing availability of substitute coverage; eliminating non-essential maintenance, and curtailing extracurricular activities.

Spending reductions of a significant magnitude result in a high level of dissatisfaction at all levels of operation. Long-term impact of a failed excess levy or reduction in regular levy rate may necessitate the reduction of professional and service positions in all budget categories. The reduction in direct services and support to students prompts significant community and staff unrest. An anticipated reduction in personnel, programs, and services may actually assist in garnering the support necessary to pass an excess levy or an increase in the regular levy rate. Whether the excess levy is eventually approved, or the regular levy rate returns to a higher level, or the funds are lost, the possibility of reduced revenue results in a major system issue and the diversion of efforts that were focused on system improvement.

Student Enrollment

Extraordinary growth or decline in student population constitutes a major issue for a school system. Most school districts funding systems are at least partially based on the number of students enrolled. Growths in enrollment may cause facility and classroom shortages, teacher shortages, and inadequate funding of immediate needs. Declining student populations may result in the need to consolidate facilities, reduce the number of employees, and reduce funds in all areas of operation.

Extraordinary growth or decline in student population requires the refocusing of administrative efforts to address the resulting issues. First, growth may result in insufficient personnel availability and inadequate classroom and facility space. To anticipate personnel and facility needs, there needs to be careful tracking of planned residential developments and business and industry relocations to the community. Currently, many school districts are experiencing shortages in certified teachers for instructional positions. In many subject areas (foreign language, advanced math and science, computer technology and special education), the teacher shortage is critical. For school districts whose population is growing, the teacher shortage is even a more difficult issue. Classroom shortages, overcrowded cafeterias, and inadequate gym and auditorium space are immediate concerns when enrollment increases. When addressing need for more classroom and facility space, school districts generally utilize one or more of the following options, each with its own set of issues that may cause staff and community concern.

First, adjustment of boundaries within a school district may be an option when addressing enrollment growths in a given area of the school district, but changing the home school of students within a district generates unrest and concern. Parents and students are concerned about the impact on academic success, extracurricular involvement, and student satisfaction.

A second option is to purchase portable classrooms. Although these classrooms provide a quick, immediate solution to overcrowded situations, a different set of issues may arise: (1) portables detract from the school attractiveness; (2) portables are often not replaced by permanent classrooms; (3) portables isolate groups of students; (4) portables magnify safety concerns with students going outside to change classrooms; and (5) portables do not address overcrowding in lunchrooms, auditorium, and gym.

A third option requires building construction. Construction of a new facility or a major addition generally requires voter approval of a bond. New construction presents its own set of issues: (1) the need to obtain voter approval; (2) the difficulty of agreeing on a site; (3) the need to possibly consolidate existing schools or populations into a new school; (4) the length of time to construct a facility; and (5) the difficulty of obtaining needed planning and staff development time and funds.

The fourth option may need to be utilized in conjunction with all the other options. It may be necessary to send students to school on alternate schedules with extended hours, perhaps dividing students into two groups, with one attending school in the morning Monday through Saturday and another attending in the afternoon. Bizarre schedules to address student enrollment increases may be proposed over the short term but are so problematic that extended use beyond a school term may turn a major issue into a crisis.

Declining enrollment generates problems that may become an ongoing major issue affecting all levels of operation in the system. Since most school district funds are tied in some form to enrollment, student population decreases mean less funds for personnel, facilities, instruction, supplies equipment, transportation, staff development, employee benefits, extracurricular activities, and substitutes. Student enrollment decline has few solutions. Without new business or industry and subsequent residential development, there are few solutions to the problems stemming from declining enrollment. School systems experiencing declining enrollment face a multitude of issues on an annual basis. Without annual reduction in staff commensurate with student decline, a school district may quickly find itself in a deficit situation. Actual reduction in force is a difficult concept. It means employees lose their jobs, and the emotional and financial issues associated with employment must be addressed. Workforce must be reduced in a prescribed manner that meets the specific personnel laws of each state. Employees are accorded due process, which involves proper notice, advisement of rights, and opportunity to be heard by the board. Reduction in force affects morale in schools, offices, and departments. Attempts are always made, and rightly so, to save the position that is proposed for reduction. Even though the idea that fewer students mean fewer personnel is understandable, it overlooks the fact that more personnel, rather than less, is usually justified. Having boards approve personnel reductions is often problematic. Boards are elected officials who represent a constituency, and reasons to negate the reduction are commonly offered. It is a well-informed, financially acute board member who understands the necessity and lack of choice in staff reductions in declining enrollments.

Declining enrollment and the accompanying revenue reduction negatively affect system operation and improvement. In addition to reducing staff and spending in all areas of operation, declining enrollment often necessitates consolidation of facilities. Unfortunately, without a bond to build a new consolidated facility or a major addition to existing buildings, consolidation results in the relocation of students to less than adequate facilities with insufficient funds to provide necessary maintenance. The school district may need to redistrict students from various schools into one school to reduce costs of operation. The consolidation may spur a multitude of overcrowding issues. Consolidation, with insufficient funds to address facility, needs usually results in inadequate programs and services for students. Without supporting new construction, consolidation simply addresses the need to have fewer buildings due to inadequate amounts of revenue.

Legislative and Congressional Mandates

At various times most state legislatures and Congress pass laws without accompanying funding. Unfunded legislative or congressional mandates affect school systems' ability to operate without going into a deficit. Implementation of unfunded legislative mandate or law may develop into a major issue for school systems. Legislative mandates should have an accompanying level of funding to ensure successful implementation and reduce the magnitude of the issue for the school system. Without sufficient funding to support the required programs, services, procedures, or staff mandated by the legislation, school systems are forced to make decisions that may reduce funding in other needed areas. Recent unfunded or partially funded mandates from the federal level include ADA disability facility requirements, EPA asbestos school rules, Title VIB least-restrictive services for special needs students, Title VIB extended school year programs, bus safety requirements, and chiller replacement requirements. State unfunded mandates are unique to each state but may include partially funded salary increases, program mandates such as full-day kindergarten, reduced pupil-teacher ratios, planning periods, staff development days, driver education, drug education and alternative schools, and increased support benefits such as workers compensation, insurance, professional and personnel leave, experience, and classification upgrades. The cost of unfunded mandates may be significant. For example, in Kanawha County Schools during the 1994–95 school year, the unfunded federal and state mandates exceeded $5 million. The following two examples highlight the impact of unfunded mandates on a school system.

Full-Day Kindergarten Programs

Research on the effect of early childhood education on academic development may motivate many states to pass legislation requiring full-day kindergarten programs for all students. The passage of legislation to require the implementation of full-day kindergarten is absolutely the right thing. Unfortunately, in some instances legal requirements for the establishment of full-day kindergarten are not accompanied by matching funds. Instituting full-day kindergarten programs is a substantial cost. Without funding for a new initiative and with limitations on any discretionary funds, school districts may be forced to realign funds from existing programs to support the mandate. Proponents of other programs may object to this reallocation or to elimination of routine increases in funding in order to support full-day kindergarten. The funding of a new mandate may cause proponents of existing programs to object to the implementation of a new initiative. The objection is not usually based on the merits of the mandate but rather on the diversion of funds from other specified programs. The concerns or objections may delay full program implementation within a school district.

Implementing full-day kindergarten may have additional issue(s) that should be addressed. Full-day kindergarten requires classroom space, which in turn may require adjusting existing programs, adding portables, or even relocating kindergarten classrooms to alternate schools with space. In addition, some parents may be concerned or unwilling to send young children to school for a full day. For them, an informational program that illustrates the benefits associated with full-day services is often beneficial. Strong emphasis on parent involvement in class and school activities may help reduce parental concern. Cost, time, and change all contribute to the degree that implementation of full-day kindergarten becomes a major issue for a school district.

Exceptional Children Mandates

Inclusion

Public Law 94-142 and subsequent supporting state policy requires that special need students be placed in the least restrictive environment. This requirement has led to inclusion of special needs students into regular classrooms. Administering special education services is difficult. Administering the "least restrictive" requirement is an on-going nightmare. The line that must be cautiously walked is between the right of the special needs student to receive an education with his or her peers within the regular classroom setting, and the right of the nonspecial needs student to receive an education without on-going disruption that may be caused by the special needs student. All too often, the answer is the addition of staff for the special needs student to remain in regular class placement. The cost for adding staff is exorbitant and often does not meet any type of reasonableness requirement. All students could benefit from the one-to-one instruction, but regular class teachers often believe there is no choice when it comes to a special needs child.

When educators are faced with a placement committee meeting consisting of attorney(s), advocates, a case-worker, and parents who are demanding inclusion, it becomes difficult to assert that inclusion is not appropriate. The discussion of inclusion is a common topic for debate at board meetings. There are no easy answers, but the notion that administrators force inclusion is not justified. A competent administrator recognizes the financial difficulties resulting from the addition of a large number of personnel to meet the inclusion needs of a small number of students. Inclusion may become a major issue for a school district without sufficient training of administrative and teaching staff to understand their role and authority in determining the best placement and defining the educational plan for special needs students. Clear and consistent interpretation of the inclusion requirement is imperative: Inclusion is not mandatory in all circumstances but only when reasonable accommodation is necessary in order for the child to benefit from the experience.

Inappropriate placement of special needs students in a regular classroom may have negative results: (1) outraged students, teacher, and parents develop their own agenda and begin attacking each other; (2) individuals running for the board use it to garner constituent groups; and (3) teacher organizations use it as a battle cry to protect members to keep special needs students in isolated classrooms. Careful decision-making regarding the placement of special needs students in regular classrooms and appropriate monitoring to ensure that the decision remains correct is important to foster appropriate inclusion opportunities. Inappropriate inclusion affects future recommendations for special needs students by breeding prejudices and/or biases in students, staff, and parents who have had negative experiences.

The inclusion of special needs students in the regular classroom is especially tricky because of the potential for board members to become involved politically in the problems or concerns related to regular class placement. Board members need to concentrate on communicating to staff their authority to make the best decisions for all children. Political involvement of board members may send the wrong message to staff and parents that central office administration is controlling the decision-making process to the detriment of "regular" students. Board members need to assist in clearly communicating the importance of appropriate inclusion. They must advocate that everyone work together to insure that decisions to include special needs students within the regular classroom are reasonable. On the issue of inclusion, it is important that board members, administrators, and teachers believe they share a common purpose as it relates to inclusion of special needs students. It is not advantageous for any group to be "for" inappropriate inclusion. The inclusion of special needs students in the regular classroom may become an on-going major issue without establishment and agreement that board, administrators, teachers, and parents work together to include students whenever it is reasonable and appropriate. Without this unified approach, the issue of special needs student inclusion may divert efforts from concentrating on moving the system forward.

Educating Special Needs Students in Their Home School

Many school districts may take the initiative to place special need students in programs within their home school rather than in cluster schools or isolated centers. This relocation of exceptional children to their home school may become a major issue for the school system. The transportation of special needs students extraordinary distances to center or cluster schools to receive instruction should be avoided. Special needs students attending clusters or centers often ride the bus for extended periods of time, which negatively affects children. Instruction in the home school is a logical recommendation that has the best interest of children in mind. Appropriate staff, programs, and services need to be relocated with the special needs students.

The placement of special needs students in their home is most frequently confused with the inclusion issue. The recommendation to return special needs students to their home school may be translated into a mandate for inclusion. Placement of a special needs student in their home school necessitates a review of the child's individual educational plan and placement of appropriate levels of staffing in the home school to accommodate the requirements of the individual educational plan. Plans should not be modified to eliminate services in order to return students to their home school. The decision, based on the requirements of PL94-142, to return students to their home school is the right one. But again, the decision to do the right thing for children may come with extraordinary complications.

Teacher organizations may view initiatives to return special needs students to their home school as an avenue to address their concerns related to inappropriate inclusion. As a result, the two issues may become confused. Individuals running for the board may respond to the issue of returning special needs students to their home school with promises of reform. Debate to establish special education county centers or cluster schools that house special needs students—versus instruction of special needs students in their home school—may occur. The return of special need students to their home school generates a mountain of board meetings discussing the pros and cons of the initiative and it creates a scapegoat for many teachers, principals, and board members complaints regarding inclusion of special need students in regular classrooms. The politicalization of the initiative to place special needs students in their home school is a disservice to children, and creates a major issue that deters the focus from system improvement.

MAJOR SYSTEM TASKS

A major system task is a report, project, and/or activity that occurs with regularity (or at least annually) and requires the effort of many administrative and support staff members to complete. Major system tasks are draining and, unfortunately, often uninteresting and laborious to complete. Any delinquency or major error in completing major tasks may have negative consequences for the school system, such as elimination or reduction funds, lack of program project approval, and/or adverse publicity.

The management structure should establish a monitoring system to ensure that major task deadlines are met. A Summary Board of Major Tasks and Deadlines needs to outline major tasks, activities, and deadlines for completion of tasks. A member of the associate team, preferably the deputy superintendent, should maintain a summary board and monitor deadlines for completion. Agendas for associate-level meetings should list tasks requiring completion, and the tasks should not be removed until completed. Without such a monitoring vehicle, due dates may be missed and a major task may turn into a major crisis and/or issue.

In deference to brevity, this chapter reviews a limited number of required tasks for such system areas as personnel, finance, facilities, instruction, and operation. The tasks are applicable to most school districts.

Federal, State, and Private Grant Application/Reports

Grant applications are applicable to most areas of system operation. School systems, depending on size and need, may receive millions of dollars in state, federal or private project money each year. For example, a school district with approximately 30,000 students, 44 percent of whom are eligible for free and reduced lunch, may receive over $5 million in funds from USDA Child Nutrition. Large projects, including child nutrition; Title I, II, IV, VI; vocational education; special education; and Eisenhower, and smaller, special project grants from state, federal, and private sources require applications. Each funding source delineates special requirements in terms of applications, reports, evaluations, on-site visits, and monitoring. Federally funded large grants generate extensive project requirements that require specialized administration to support personnel, programming, and services and to secure continuous funding. Small grants also require coordination, development, and management. All new project money should support system objectives and activities in order to secure necessary financial support.

Ideally, one administrator should serve as the clearinghouse or point person for all applications and projects that are submitted. The project administrator should: (1) secure and disseminate information on sources for potential funding; (2) assist in actual grant writing; and (3) review all applications prior to submission to funding agency. All project initiatives should be reviewed in order to determine that: (1) the system financial officer reviewed the budget, approved any commitment of local dollars, and included any indirect costs; (2) the application supports system objectives; and (3) the application establishes a process to monitor compliance with required submission deadlines. Investment in an administrative position to manage projects and applications should result in increased special funding availability for system improvements. Without an administrator to motivate, coordinate, and monitor project development, submission, and implementation, it is difficult to secure a significant level of grant awards and to effectively manage all the tasks related to special project requirements. A school district's investment in a position to seek and manage submission of grants should pay off in needed funding for projects and initiatives in all areas of the system. Otherwise, missing deadlines for submission of applications or completion of required reports may result in front-page headlines, and a major task may become a major issue if not properly managed.

State-Required Project Submissions

Local school districts are required to submit numerous projects and reports to state agencies. The reports generally require comprehensive involvement of individuals throughout the system, and almost always require board approval prior to submission. The coordination of project submissions is generally the responsibility of the lead administrator for the department with the greatest involvement. The projects often require the coordination of efforts between and among divisions, departments, and offices. The following examples of state-required submissions are applicable to most school districts.

Comprehensive Educational Facility Plans (CEFP)

Most states require local education agencies to develop and submit a comprehensive educational facility plan. The development of a comprehensive facility plan requires the review of facility needs in light of educational and health and safety requirements. An update of the facility plan is usually completed annually, and a new comprehensive plan is completed every five to ten years. The plan's development is a complicated, highly technical process requiring intensive involvement from each school in the system and their respective communities. In addition, a facility plan requires a high level of technical and administrative expertise in coordinating involvement, evaluating facility needs, and determining cost estimates for repair, renovation, and new construction. The development of a comprehensive facility plan is a frustrating, multiyear process that usually requires some type of referendum for funding, such as a bond issue or state legislation. Bond issues are difficult to obtain. The enormous amount of work required to develop the facility plan is often completed without facility improvement taking place. At the same time, the issues involved in facility plan development are rife with controversy. Discussions of schools to be renovated, replaced, or closed are difficult and may easily turn the plan's development from a major task to a major issue.

Major Facility Improvement Projects

States often establish funds for major facility improvement projects at the local level. The dollars are usually limited and funding is highly competitive. Local school districts develop and submit to the state projects for specific renovation or improvement to a school(s), such as additional classrooms to meet student enrollments needs, replacement of HVAC systems, additional gymnasiums, or enlarged cafeterias. Applications for building projects may cause turmoil because the number of schools needing repair or renovation exceeds funding. State funds are usually limited and fund awards are restricted in number and amount. Considerable time is needed to develop these applications and funds are often not approved. It is politically disastrous not to seek funds, but it is often an exercise in futility.

Enrollment and Personnel Reports

In most school districts, distribution of state funds is based upon student enrollment. The submission of reports verifying number of service and professional personnel and the number of students on a given date is a critical task that must be completed by local school districts. The reports are usually mandatory for continued state funding for the school system. These reports are submitted to the state and include the following:

Professional/Service Personnel Report. Most school districts are required to submit a personnel report documenting placement, location, certification of teachers, and number of students served by each employee assigned to a position. Failure to maintain properly certified individuals in vacant positions affects the number of personnel for which the school district receives reimbursement. Administrators at the school level and at the central office must coordinate the completion of this report. A top-notch certification analyst is necessary to ensure that only properly certified or permitted individuals are assigned to positions. Administrators must also ensure that all employed individuals are properly assigned to a position and that vacant positions are filled with substitutes prior to submission of the report. Failure to properly monitor that all vacant positions are assigned a substitute may result in unfunded positions for the following year.

Student Count Report. An annual count of all students in the school system is a report usually required for submission to the state on a specified date each year. Most states' reimbursement systems are directly tied to student enrollment. A decline in student enrollment in a school district corresponds with a decline in number of positions funded and revenue received from the state. Student enrollment count usually includes the net enrollment at the end of a specific month of school plus the number of special needs students receiving services. The two numbers are calculated to arrive at a school district's adjusted enrollment. The adjusted enrollment is then used to determine the level of state aid to the school system. Therefore, accurate counting and reporting of data is critical to funding. Elementary and secondary schools complete reporting forms based on enrollment figures, and county administrators garner information on special education enrollment to submit an accurate completed report to the state department of education.

Vocational Education Plan

States that receive federal aid through the Carl Perkins Act for vocational programs require local school districts to submit a comprehensive vocational plan annually. The plan outlines vocational objectives, activities, and funding needs and requires a review of all vocational programs and a determination of programs that need to be continued, revised, or eliminated. The plan also includes the development of plans for program expansion. The award of state dollars for vocational education to local school districts is based on an approved local plan for vocational education. Funding of the vocational education plan supports programs in all secondary schools and vocational centers. System objectives designed to improve the delivery and type of vocational services are eligible to receive necessary financial support through this vocation plan.

District Special Educational Plan.

Title VIB regulations require local school districts to submit a comprehensive special education plan to the state. The plan outlines special education needs, objectives, staffing, and funding requests. The district special education plan is submitted annually to the state. The comprehensive plan outlines the need for continuation, change, and expansion of special needs programs. Receipt of federal and state funds is based on an approved county special education plan. Appropriate and thoughtful development of this special education plan may help support necessary programs for special needs students and the development of innovative approaches for program improvement. Coordination in the development of system objectives that improve special education services may result in needed financial support for the special education plan.

Requirements for submission of projects to the state pertain to almost every department within the school system. Personnel, transportation, food service, finance, accounting facilities, and instructional reports are routinely submitted to the state. These require time to complete, review, and obtain necessary administrative and board approval. All reports should be developed and reviewed to ensure coordination or support as it relates to system objectives.

The associate team should coordinate submission of all special reports and projects. Department heads should submit a listing of all reports required for submission and the corresponding due dates. Reports should be included in the Summary Board of Major Tasks and Deadlines, and a member of the associate team should compile and monitor the chart of known projects and report submissions and corresponding due dates. Department heads should be required to notify the "coordinator of reports" when specified reports are submitted. The summary board chart should be posted in a conference room where it is visible to all administrators.

State Accreditation Process

Local school districts must comply with some type of state accreditation process. Generally, states develop standards for accreditation. Local school districts are required to verify their level of compliance with each standard. A state monitoring system is usually in place that includes a scheduled on-site review of the school district. In preparation for on-site visits, school districts should annually review all operational and program areas. This review ensures that schools and the school district meet accreditation standards and collects all necessary verification for an audit of the school system. A review of all operating functions (personnel, instruction, student performance, transportation, food service, facilities, maintenance, budget, and finance) of the school system and schools must be completed based on established standards provided by the state. Periodically, a state conducts on-site visits to review all written documentation and to verify evidence by observing offices, classrooms, and schools.

Breaking down the component requirements in the accreditation process to accountable or manageable units is imperative. Each administrator at the local and county level should understand and maintain records verifying compliance against applicable requirements. Much pain may be averted by assigning coordination for disseminating requirements to managers and maintenance of verifiable data to a single responsible central office administrator.

Budget Construction

The on-going process of budget construction begins with each new fiscal year and is completed only a few months prior to the end of the fiscal year. Budgets are usually approved at a statutory session of the board and submitted to the state for approval before the end of the current fiscal year. The budget process is a complicated, multifaceted procedure that may become increasingly complex with significant involvement from constituent groups throughout the system and if funding requests exceed anticipated funding levels. In developing the budget, input from the building level on needs and priorities should be secured. The budget should reflect the funding of priority items within budget constraints. A review of the system objectives and alignment of needed funds should take place during the development of a system's budget. A commitment to local school-based decision-making requires that supporting funds accompany the decision-making responsibility. The level of commitment to site-based decision-making is validated when actual dollars flow to directly to individual schools.

Staffing formulas that determine need are imperative in the budget development process. Without staffing formulas for personnel, teachers, service personnel and administrators, personnel, allocation may become arbitrary. Staffing schools without prescribed formulas or procedures often puts schools in competition with each other, demanding more positions because "school y" has this position and "school x" does not.

The budget construction process needs to be driven by two separate elements: number of positions supported by state and local revenues and identified system objectives. The first element affects the entire budget construction process. As enrollment, regular, or excess levy revenues decline or increase, the level of funds to support positions increases or decreases. The development of system objectives requires that individual schools review statistical and factual data to determine need. The objectives establish specific work objectives or activities necessary to accomplish the objective. The system objectives often involve a significant level of funding. The cost for funding required service and professional positions and system objectives is a primary element for consideration in the budget process. Any known unfunded mandates, either legislative or judicial, should also be considered. (Chapter 3 provides detailed information on funding mechanisms and requirements that need to be considered in the budget construction process.)

The budget construction process is often controversial because it directly relates to the number and type of jobs funded for the next school year. The process therefore includes properly notifying individuals who must be transferred or reduced in force. The budget process should adhere to statutory requirements on notification and hearing opportunities for affected individuals. Personnel hearings usually cover a two-month period. Depending on the number of personnel changes, personnel hearings may consume ten to twenty days of the superintendent's and other administrators' time.

State statutes usually require submission of a balanced budget to the state department of education. A preliminary budget must be approved by the board in a statutory hearing and then submitted to the state for approval. The proposed budget may require the arbitrary elimination of known expenses with the anticipation of a carry-over balance to support expenses during the next fiscal year. Without a carry-over balance and with declining revenues, the possibility of creating a deficit situation increases. Carry-over balances are determined after all bills for a fiscal year are paid. At this point, the school system's fiscal condition is clearer. Unfunded items eliminated from the proposed budget are re-considered after a carry-over balance is determined.

Transportation Schedules

Comprehensive transportation schedules, developed annually, are based on a comprehensive review of students' addresses, number of buses, and required instructional minutes for each school. This annual development of transportation schedules may be problematic if there are significant time or route changes. Any significant change in transportation schedules may cause outcry from students, parents, and school personnel. Parents and teachers are accustomed to certain arrival and dismissal times, and any change causes dissatisfaction from some constituency group. Implementing comprehensive transportation changes is guaranteed to trigger student, parent, and employee concern.

The development of a comprehensive transportation schedules using a data-based system is more efficient and cost-effective. Transportation software that is linked to student computer data information is an efficient and manageable transportation system. A data-based transportation system requires a comprehensive annual update because students change school locations, but it also requires daily updating to maintain current student addresses and transportation schedules. The computerization of transportation schedules enhances bus transportation efficiency and safety, but requires a commitment to annually complete a major update along with adherence to a process for making continuous changes. Additional use of transportation software data includes the quick dissemination of essential information regarding students in emergency situations and for maximizing facility usage.

Summer School

Most school districts offer some minimal level of summer school opportunities for high school students to make up specific course credit requirements. In addition to secondary summer school for high school students, school districts are required to offer extended year programs for special needs students. Summer high school and extended year programs are annually developed and managed. The development of plans for secondary summer school and the variety of summer extended year programs includes the designation of specific programs to be offered and personnel required, identification and enrollment of students to be served, and coordination of transportation schedules and food services. Plans for the secondary summer school and extended year programs are developed and submitted for approval to the state department.

To provide additional time for learning and enhance program flexibility, school districts are striving to increase the number and types of summer programs available for students: Title I remedial schools, summer foreign language institutes, enrichment programs for music and art, honor academies, and alternative high schools. Enhanced summer learning programs require school districts to engage in annual comprehensive planning and continuous management support activities.

Staff Development

A comprehensive staff development plan is a necessary element of system improvement plans. Staff development plans should define types of programs required, target audiences, and timeframe for implementation of training programs, and should be coordinated with the system objectives and activities. A five-year staff development plan should be developed with annual updates that include specific plans for programming during the entire school year and summer. The plan for staff development includes specific opportunities and requirements in four major component areas: (1) school-based staff development; (2) system-wide staff development; (3) technology staff development; and (4) restructuring and reforming staff development. Topics for school-based staff development should include but are not limited to budgeting, monitoring, strategic planning, teaming and peer coaching, school-based assistant teams, instructional strategies, cooperative learning, effective school correlates, High Schools That Work, state standards, rationale discipline, inclusion, and whole language. On-going system-wide staff development should focus on training entire staffs on site-based decision-making, instructional strategies, higher standards, minimum requirements, diversity, community service learning, mentorships, secondary restructuring initiatives, middle school strategies, and students' education plans. The technology staff development component should be updated annually to address continued innovations. Areas emphasized for technology training should include student information-based systems, Internet, school-based software packages, Windows software, desktop publishing, and multimedia applications. Finally, staff development training should support comprehensive restructuring efforts in elementary and secondary schools. The appropriate staff development to support recommendations for restructuring should be incorporated into total school training opportunities, administrative conferences and meetings, school department level meetings, and faculty staff meetings. Leadership academies and specific program area conferences should support training necessary to implement recommendations of restructuring committees. Staff development plans should establish and maintain cadres of teachers who provide training and support to schools throughout the year in many of the following areas:

TESA	Instructional learning strategies
Multiple intelligence	Peer coaching
SAP	Cooperative learning
GEMS	Cooperative discipline
AIMS	Critical thinking
K-3 Math	Inclusion
QUILT	Internet
Rationale discipline	Whole language

The commitment to staff development requires a multitude of special class offerings and workshops for professional and service personnel. Funding is extremely important to comprehensive staff development. Direct allocations should be provided to schools for staff development, and funds allocated for system-wide staff development should meet the needs identified in the comprehensive staff development plan.

Planning for summer staff development is an annual endeavor that requires enormous amounts of time in development and implementation. Plans should include preparation for an annual teacher's academy, leadership academy, new school or consolidated school training, middle school conversion training, whole school training on instructional strategies, and restructuring or any other specific initiative, such as converting junior highs to middle schools, four-by-four scheduling, and the international baccalaureate program.

Surplus Property

If a school system's enrollment is declining, or if there is new school construction, the number of empty buildings may multiply over time. Vacant school properties should be inventoried with an eye toward liquidating property, if necessary. Vacant school buildings often may not be the most desirable pieces of property, or may not be found in prime locations. Developing a property liquidation process that complies with legal requirements and allows for successful competition in the real-estate market is challenging. The use of real-estate companies and local nonprofit business and industrial councils may result in the successful disposition of vacant school property. The sale of property makes available additional dollars for needed permanent improvement projects. In addition, disposal of vacant property is important for maintaining community support. A vacant school building in a community detracts from property values. Proper management of surplus property on an annual basis may help garner voter approval of bonds to support capital improvement projects.

District Safe School Plan

Safety is a major concern of most school systems. Most states require school districts to develop an annual district-wide safe school plan. A prudent safe school plan, that considers the specifics of each individual school and is feasible to implement, is essential. A comprehensive district-wide safe school committee should be formed that: (1) reviews and makes recommendations for individual safe school plans at the building level; (2) recommends implementation of specific system-wide safety procedures; and (3) develops recommendations for needed alternative education programs and schools.

Each school should develop a school-wide safe school plan with input from all constituent groups: students, teachers, service personnel, parents, and community representatives. Individual school plans that specify identified needs, objectives, activities, and recommendations should be submitted to the district-wide safe school committee. That committee should then generate an annual plan that includes:

1. Specific safe school procedures at the school level;
2. Specific support systems for addressing behavior issues at the local level, such as counselors, psychologists, school-based assistant teams, advisors, peer counselors, and so on; and
3. Alternative education programs, such as evening school, alternative time schedules, alternative schools, computer-based instruction programs, and home-bound instruction.

Annual School and District Education Improvement Plan

The development of annual school and school district education improvement plans are generally part of a state accreditation process. The school and district improvement plans are usually developed annually and submitted to the state for approval. The annual school and county education plan should be developed and coordinated with the management system improvement process. Each school should review pertinent data and develop objectives and activities for the school education improvement plan. The school district should then combine the local school plans into a comprehensive district plan for educational improvement that includes objectives and activities. The county education improvement plan is a major part of a comprehensive system improvement process.

State Testing Program

School districts are involved in the administration and coordination of an annual comprehensive testing program. The testing includes such instruments as the Stanford 9 in grades two through eleven; Writing Assessment in grades four, seven, and ten; ACT Explore in grade eight; ACT Plan in grade ten; PSAT in grades ten and eleven; ACT in grades eleven and twelve; and Work Keys in grade twelve. The administration of these various instruments is just one part of a testing program. Coordinating preparation programs, training staff, ordering materials, disseminating tests, monitoring test security, interpreting test results, and utilizing test information in program planning are all tasks of the testing program that should be completed annually. Standardized testing programs may turn into a crisis if any one of the component parts breaks down. Lack of proper student preparation, test security and administration mistakes, and test score decline are "breakdowns" in the testing program process that cause great concern.

DAILY CRISIS

Almost without exception, it is an unusual day in a large school system if an event does not occur that is considered a crisis. Perhaps the number of daily crises is attributable to the following: (1) the stressful world in which we all reside; (2) the aging work force in teacher education; (3) the deteriorating family; (4) the lack of dollars for facility upkeep in this century; and (5) even El Niño.

Whatever the reason, the ability to deal with a continual onslaught of crisis situations demands a fairly high level of tolerance for living with circumstances beyond your control. *Webster* defines crisis as a crucial time (Saukhanou 1998, 328). The definition holds true for the magnitude of occurrences within a school system that can be defined as a crisis. A level of preparedness is absolutely essential for withstanding this category of occurrences. Items in this category may begin as a problem but quickly escalate to a crisis, depending on the degree of involvement in the issues by students, parents, staff, community members, or board members. Once their involvement grows, situations not defined initially as crisis may be made into one. The number of daily crises may be reduced with enough forethought, and all crises may be brought to a reasonable conclusion with enough perseverance and communication. Understanding this daily crisis category is an important part of understanding the complexities of a school system. Types of crises are grouped into the following categories: (1) personnel; (2) facility; (3) environmental; (4) student; and (5) policy and procedure.

Personnel

Staffing Requests/Demand

Students move in and out of schools daily, and this affects staffing. Without the necessary procedures, requests for additional staff may escalate to a crisis. A crowded classroom or a classroom with a difficult child may become intolerable with the addition of one more child. The process usually begins with phone calls made to teacher organizations or to board members. The superintendent receives calls demanding the immediate assignment of an additional teacher. It is imperative that a structured process is in place for determining staffing adjustments or chaos reigns. Having area assistant superintendents located in schools provides a calming, problem-solving effect on such demands for more staff. Area assistant superintendents should be required to review all requests and make recommendations prior to the addition of staff. This process keeps this potential crisis area manageable, even though stressful. Many times demands for staff may end up as a news item. Parents and teachers may call the media if a staff addition is not immediate. Staffing adjustments must be made with consideration of its impact system-wide. If a classroom of thirteen students is staffed with a teacher and an aide, it sets a precedent for all other classes with thirteen students to request the same staffing.

Job Selection

The superintendent is responsible for recommending all personnel for employment or job assignments. Personnel selection is almost a no-win situation. In almost every job vacancy, there is an individual who is not recommended for the job. At least one individual is always dissatisfied. Administrative jobs are particularly nightmarish. When an individual recommended for a principal's position is not the individual a given board member wants, it is particularly difficult. Knowledgeable, sophisticated board members stay out of the personnel placement process. Board members need to communicate to their constituency that they have no authority to recommend an individual for employment. However, some board members find the personnel selection process difficult to resist. Other members of the community who desire a certain individual for a principal position may wage a campaign for that individual with telephone calls, letters, and board appearances.

Personnel selection is of the utmost importance to the success of a school system. It serves no good purpose to select an individual who is less than the most competent applicant for a position. It is imperative that superintendents remain committed to the selection of the most qualified individuals for all positions and not be swayed by political pressure. A superintendent's success in employing the most qualified individual is directly related to his or her willingness to take on a level of crisis generated by those who want someone else. Doing what is right for children is most important, and what is right is selecting the best and brightest individual for the position.

Staff Conduct

Staff conduct is a category that seems to be growing at a rate faster than most school systems' legal counsel is able to handle. Staff misconduct usually includes the following categories: sexual abuse; physical abuse; neglect; insubordination; and incompetence. Misconduct by staff is almost always fodder for newspaper articles and nightly news feature stories. Specific staff misconduct is truly endless: personnel accused of physical abuse (hitting, kicking, biting, and so on); personnel accused of sexual abuse of their students (dating, molestation, or prostitution); personnel engaged in deviant sexual behavior outside of school (being arrested always brings it to the forefront); personnel using or distributing drugs; personnel losing students; personnel engaged in sexual harassment of fellow employees; and personnel smoking or drinking.

Incompetence is also included under conduct. Generally one sees three types of incompetence. The first type is that brought on by years of burn-out in addition to mediocre teaching and/or service ability. Retirement is a viable alternative for this type of incompetence because remediation is almost impossible. Young teachers who graduate from college unprepared with basic classroom management skills and poor understanding of content generally compose the second type of incompetence. The third type consists of those who don't or won't put forth the level of effort required to be successful as a teacher, service staff member, or administrator.

As efforts increase to monitor local performance, more individuals are usually placed on plans of improvement. Without exception, formalizing efforts to require teachers and administrators to improve or move on increases dissatisfaction at many levels. This level of personnel accountability may result in school, community, and/or board member unrest. No matter how "disfunctional" an employee may be, there is always a constituency willing to voice opposition to efforts of accountability. Likewise, not addressing a "disfunctional" employee results in a different constituency voicing concerns. Either way a crisis is always looming.

Accident, Illness, and Death

Personnel are frequently involved in an accident, sustain an injury, become critically ill, or die at school or outside of school. When this happens it is not only the individual employee who is affected; students and communities react and need to be supported. Students attachment to a favorite teacher or principal who is with them one day and gone the next brings much emotional conflict. Students at all school levels feel a sense of loss and injustice when someone is hurt or dies. Staff and community members are also affected. A crisis intervention team needs to help students and staff deal with emotionally charged situations. A good crisis team consists of specifically trained counselors, school psychologists, and social workers and administrators who can provide necessary comfort and support.

Facility

Weather-Related

Flood, snow, ice, and extreme cold and heat affects a facility's operation. Weather-related facility emergencies, which often occur while students are in school, require relocating students to fix the building problem. If the building damage occurs late at night, it requires a decision in the early hours of morning about whether to open or close the school. Flooding may cause significant damage to schools. Organizing the level of building and grounds repair required and assuring that it is done in the quickest manner possible is imperative. Constant progress updates to the students, parents, and public about facility repair is imperative.

Health and Safety-Related

Asbestos problems, air quality, water stoppage, fires, boiler explosions, and heating and air conditioning system breakdowns all occur. Serious health and safety-related facility not only require dealing with remedies, but may involve long-term litigation when students or staff believe they have been subjected to a health or safety hazard. Buildings constructed in the 1960s, with few windows and open space design, which were subsequently converted to standard classrooms, are often faced with air quality problems. This is indicative of past design problems that school systems of today must face.

Environmental

Weather

Inclement weather seems to begin in the middle of the night. A bad winter is an extended bad nightmare for a superintendent. Cold temperatures and ice and snow all require decisions about whether to have school, whether to delay school, whether to call employees out, and/or whether to have employees come out on a two-hour delay. Whatever decision is made, it is wrong in someone's mind. A school cancellation or delay in opening based upon inclement weather prompts a day full of phone calls with people giving their opinion about the decision. Weather problems that occur during the day require stopping everything else to determine what is the best decision to keep students safe. (When will the storm hit? Is it better to dismiss students now or keep them until after the storm?) A recommendation from both the national weather bureau and the department of highways is preferential before making a final decision. (The recommendation may not be correct, but it is far superior to make a decision based on the advice of experts about the weather and road conditions than on what someone "thinks.") It is important to press the national weather service for a recommendation and to document whatever information it communicates. Department of highways should be contacted to determine the condition of roads, projected management of the storm, and recommendation for school opening or closing.

The logistics of managing extreme amounts of snow or cold weather is extraordinary and not taught in any administration class. Clearing three feet of snow at different building locations within a school system is a daunting and expensive undertaking. School systems generally do not have sufficient personnel to clear the parking lots to accommodate staff within a short timeframe. Highways are often clear before schools may reopen. Extreme cold weather is also problematic. If schools are open when the temperature is below zero, parents become angry. Severe hot temperatures bring their own set of problems. If all the buildings are not air-conditioned and temperatures soar to the mid-90s, student and facility problems develop: heat-related illnesses often occur; students find it difficult to concentrate, and everyone is angry because they are inside a hot building. Generally, when the heat index hits 90 degrees, schools need to be dismissed. It is ironic that even though citizens complain about hot buildings, bonds to air-condition buildings are often defeated.

In school districts that are large and geographically diverse, the weather can be bad in part of the district and satisfactory in another area. Coordination of transportation schedules makes opening and closing a certain set of schools almost impossible. Staff may work in a school that is not experiencing bad weather, but they live where it has just flooded or there is six inches of snow.

Chemical Leak/Spill

A chemical leak or spill is always a possibility within a community. Major highways and railroads transverse school districts. Tractor-trailers and or trains carrying chemicals may wreck and cause major spills, or a chemical leak from a plant may occur. When a chemical leak occurs, contact between emergency services and the affected schools is necessary. Emergency service directs whether schools shelter in place or evacuate. Communication is a major problem with an environmental crisis. First, obtaining correct direction from emergency service departments may take considerable time if all the information regarding the spill has not been provided to emergency service in a timely manner. Schools are anxious to know what to do and frequent calls/communication are necessary to keep everyone calm. Concerned parents also want to know "right now" what is happening. Second, coordination of any evacuation efforts through the transportation department is of prime importance. Blocked roads may make it impossible or very difficult to get buses to the affected schools. The situation also frequently changes as emergency departments learn more about the leak or spill. In a matter of minutes, one may go from a directive to shelter in place to evacuation . Effective communication devices become essential. Have available dedicated emergency phone lines, plexons, portable phone access, walkie-talkies, and pagers in every school.

Students

Academic

Students frequently have academic problems. However, when a few key factors are present, academic problems may become a crisis. If it is spring and grade-ranking is taking place, then interpretation of various policies regarding credited courses may mean the difference between valedictorian and salutatorian. For example, parents might not understand that in some school districts, an algebra course taken in eighth grade counts in the student's high-school grade-point average. Academic problems may become a crisis if the star football or basketball player does not make the grade-point average necessary to remain eligible for sports. Additionally, a crisis may result if accusations of grade changes take place. With higher standards and more accountability, school systems face increased academic issues that may develop into a crisis.

Disciplinary

Students and parents often contend that student misbehavior is not the student's fault because it stems from unfair or prejudicial treatment by the teacher or principal. Arguments that question due process procedures and disciplinary actions are common in most school systems. Suspensions from schools may make the news. For example, a suspension of a student for allegedly taking a cough drop has made national news. As Paul Harvey would say, "That's not the end of the story." Since discussion of a student's disciplinary record with the media is not appropriate, often only one side of the story can be presented. In an era of concern about safety in schools, disciplining students who are perceived to be dangerous is often controversial. Ensuring due process may be difficult when there are demands for a student's immediate removal or exclusion of a student.

Weapon-Related

A student who brings a weapon (pocket knife, razor blade, look-alike gun, or any device capable of inflicting harm) to school creates a crisis. First, ensuring everyone's safety is of utmost importance. Police are typically involved, and the media demand details. Staff and parents of other students simply want the student out of the school. Second, preserving the student's due process rights and fundamental right to an education, and at the same time preventing panic in the local school must be carefully handled. All students must be accorded a hearing. Student disciplinary cases are frequently taken to court. Legal arguments generally relate to intent to harm and whether a weapon is a weapon (is a pipe or a fork a weapon?). Weapon cases generally require a hard line about consistent punishment. Students who bring weapons need to be removed from the regular school setting for a period of time. However, alternative education services must be considered when a student is excluded from regular school. The alternative education options may include on-line computer instruction, home-bound instruction, or placement in an alternative school. A hard-line, zero tolerance approach should result in fewer weapon cases.

Special Education

Special needs students who have multiple disorders and whose individual education plan requires inclusion in a regular classroom may create a crisis. The crisis may be generated because the classroom teacher or the parents of regular education students believe the level of special educator support is not sufficient. Even when a special instructor or aide is assigned to the special needs student, if the behavior is disruptive or bizarre, tensions may escalate within the regular classroom. Particularly problematic is placement of autistic students in the regular classroom. Autistic behavior is often distracting and objectionable to the regular class teacher. Placement of students with acting-out behaviors may escalate the issue in the press or the board.

Answers are not easy, because there must be a balance between the special needs student's right to an education with his or her peers and a regular class student's right to an education free of major distractions. The amount of support staff required for a special needs student is often substantial. Parents who disagree with the level of service provided by the local school district may file a grievance with the state department of education. All too often the disposition of the case requires additional staff or services in order to reduce conflict and or controversy. There is often a lack of reasonableness in the provision of additional special education services.

Accident/Illness/Death

It is always traumatic when a student hurt, is terminally ill, or dies. The tragedy affects both the student and classmates. Car wrecks, murders, suicides, and crippling accidents all occur with increasing regularity. An established crisis intervention team should be in place to help schools deal with the emotional issues. The crisis intervention team should be composed of counselors, school psychologists, social workers, and administrators with training in crisis management and student support.

Policy and/or Procedure Related

Policy and procedural-related crises are those developing from complaints that the school district did not follow board policy or procedures correctly or that specific policy or procedures violate someone's rights. Many school districts are the major purchaser of goods and services within their community. Companies who are not awarded a contract may create problems. The size of the contract determines the level of crisis that can be generated. Companies or individuals not receiving the award contend that they better met the bid's specifications and that the school system violated proper purchasing practices. Companies who are not awarded a contract may contact the funding agency if it is a special project or contact board members to complain of unfair treatment. The potential for a crisis is minimized if purchasing processes are clearly defined and a sufficient number of capable administrators monitor adherence to purchasing procedures. Development of accurate specifications, compliance with all bid requirements, and adherence to the low bidder preference are key to avoid conflict with companies. In most instances, if clear procedures are in place and adequately monitored when a company objects to not receiving a contract, a review of the procedures with the company, objecting agency, and/or board members brings resolution, or at least acceptance of the decision. Resolution is often contingent on demonstration that procedures are correctly followed.

Religion may be a close second to purchasing problems in ability to cause a crisis. The constitution and board policy, supported by case law, prohibit religion in schools. The number and type of activities to circumvent the separation of church and state requirement are mind-boggling.

With each ruling made by administration to abide by the policy/law, turmoil is possible. Prayer at graduation, religious clubs, prayer at ball games, prayer at board meetings, distribution of Bibles, Crusade for Christ (athletic-sponsored organization) are just a few of the religious issues that periodically must be addressed. Civil libertarian groups monitor school systems as it relates to religion in the public schools. Consistency is important in all responses to religious issues. Reliance on case law is a must and avoiding personal interpretation of the question is essential. Assistance from any other agency, such as the state department, is often refused or avoided in deference to a decision that might initiate a problem in another school district.

SUMMARY

Understanding the complexities of the daily operation of a school system is essential to "keeping the train on the track and peace in the valley." School system operation is one of the two main functions of a school management system; the other is school system improvement. However, operation may be the only major endeavor that a management system addresses if an effective management system and system improvement process are not defined, supported, and implemented. A strong management system ensures the level of accountability necessary for the daily system operation and ensures coordination with system improvement initiatives. Clear system objectives, developed within an improvement process, guide administrative decisions and actions as the daily concerns, tasks, issues, and crises are addressed.

System operation may be categorized into three concerns: major issues, major tasks, and daily crises. It is important to understand the areas of concern in order to understand the necessity for establishing a quality management and improvement system. School system operation is complex and demanding. Daily operation is filled with enough diversions to prevent the implementation of any comprehensive plan for system improvement. Without a structured plan for improving the system, a school district may only be able to address the task, issue, and crisis of the day. Author Stephen Covey provides guidance to administrators on how to handle daily tasks/issues/crisis. Covey warns that it is easy to become weighted down by daily concerns, and the goals and objectives for moving the system forward may become lost. Covey sites examples of athletes who are trained to maintain their focus. In very tense moments, if athletes don't maintain their focus, they become overwhelmed by the immediate rather than consumed with achieving their goal of winning the game (Covey 1994, 84). An effective management system should address the daily operation requirements and implement a comprehensive system improvement plan for efficient school system operation.

CHAPTER 5

Conclusions

Knowledge. says Bacon, is power; but mere knowledge is not
power; it is only possibility. Action is power; and its highest
manifestation is when it is directed by knowledge.

—T. W. PALMER (BROWNS, 332)

When core components, minimum organizational requirements, a management system, and an improvement process are established and committed to up front, then there is a clearer awareness of role and
responsibilities and a greater opportunity for marked progress. Superintendents need to generate position papers that clearly articulate plans for
establishing core components for making school systems work. Preferably, the position papers should be developed prior to the beginning of
the superintendent's term of office. A precontract period of at least three
months enables the superintendent-elect to generate the position papers.
Boards need to formally approve and support minimum organizational
requirements, a management system, and an improvement process,
either in the superintendent's contract or in board policy.

If school systems are going to work, there needs to be more clarity
and less rhetoric by those involved in the education process. Clarity may
be improved by developing greater understanding of all aspects of school
system operation, minimum requirements, management, and improvement. School systems are complex organizations that require understanding, commitment, and a level of accountability that is organized and
comprehensive. The complexity of school systems make it imperative
that the components defined for making the school system work are
established, communicated, understood, and supported.

Commitment to implementation of minimum organizational requirements, a comprehensive management system, and an improvement
process is not short term. Schlechty (1997) repeatedly addresses the
importance of commitment. This commitment is essential because

133

systemic changes take time—there is no quick fix in education. Institutionalization of system change takes years. It takes time to plan, implement, and continue the changes over a substantial period before they become a way of operation (Kaufman and Zahn 1983, 8).

Commitment should not be freely given without a tangible document for what is expected to be achieved in a school system. The public and the board should require the superintendent to provide plans that (1) detail personnel and programmatic structures that need to be in place in schools and the school system—minimum organizational requirements; (2) establish the administrative organizational structure to manage all aspects of the school system—management system; and (3) develop the structures necessary to bring about school and system progress—improvement process. Minimum organizational structures, a management system, and an improvement process that includes school and system objectives must be defined, articulated, and acted on by administrators, with opportunity for employee input. If tangible plans for implementation of each core component are in place, it is fair to expect long-term support and commitment from the board and the community.

In a "quick fix" society, bringing about system change is problematic. Without written plans and established support, efforts to bring about positive change are greatly weakened. The "calling card" for individuals running for boards is too often based on "throw out the rascals" mentality. This type of politicization of boards is a major factor in the evolution of school system mediocrity.

Boards that function as a "board of directors" understand there are no fast "fix-its" for school systems, and reflect, think, and commit to long-term restructuring. Boards that function as a true policy-making body demonstrate the greatest potential to improve education (Thompson 1994, 5). Unfortunately most boards' concerns hinder system reform (Silver 1998, 3). Making school systems work by developing understandings and commitments that foster accountability in boards, superintendents, employees, and the community is fundamental to school and school system success.

If administrators and educators are held accountable for their performance, communities and boards need to assume a level of responsibility for supporting public education Board and community responsibility to public education requires more than words; it requires boards who are willing to build consensus in the community for the monetary needs of a school system.

Making School Systems Work builds on an acceptance by the community and the board of their responsibilities to be "for" public education. Developing necessary understanding and commitments is easier when boards and communities acknowledge their responsibilities in a democracy to building community consensus to support public education. The operation and improvement of school systems becomes more attainable if components for making school systems result in the:

1. Establishment of a defined, agreed-upon minimum organizational structure for elementary schools, secondary school and central office administration.

2. Establishment of a management system that (a) efficiently and effectively addresses the tasks, issues and crises that occur in the daily operation of the school system; (b) specifies a plan for monitoring accountability of employees and students by defining expectation, such as student minimum requirements, employee standards for performance, and limiting span of control of employees per supervisor in keeping with business and industry standards; (c) defines a communication plan that provides opportunities to receive and give information from all constituency groups; and (d) brings about comprehensive system improvement.

3. Establishment of a defined process for bringing about system improvement that includes (a) commitment to using statistical tools to gather data to ascertain need and to determine how much progress occurs; (b) commitment to secure input from all entities affected—students, parents, teachers, service personnel, administrators, business, industry, and community members; (c) commitment of each individual to their own ability and desire to make a difference in system improvement; (d) commitment to understand one's own responsibility to work together in a forthright, caring manner; (e) commitment to annually define system school, office, and department objectives; and (f) commitment to annually assess level of progress in implementing system (focus and work) objectives.

4. Establishment of a process for educating all employees, boards, and the community on school system operation, including issues, tasks, and crises that must be addressed on a daily basis.

Establishment of the core components, minimum organizational requirements, a management system, and an improvement process must be cooperatively implemented and supported by superintendents, boards, administrators, teachers, service personnel, and the community as they work for the efficient and effective daily operation of the school system. This will "keep the train on the track." As they work for positive improvement in all areas of operation, they will lay new track," and as they work together in harmonious commitment to doing what is best for children, they will "keep peace in the valley."

> "Let us put our minds together and see what life
> we can make for our children."
>
> —SITTING BULL, A LAKOTA SIOUX,
> QUOTED IN ERNEST BOYER, *THE BASIC SCHOOL*

APPENDIX A

Source Information for Minimum Organizational Requirements

ACADEMIC ADVISORS

1. The identification process for Blue Ribbon High Schools requires verification that all students have access to mentor or advisor programs that assist with school work, career exploration and preparation for college. www.ed.gov/offices/OERI/BlueRibbon Schools/2001-2002nompackage.doc.

ACCELERATED READING PROGRAM

1. McKnight found in a study of a fifth-grade class that more than one half of students who lacked motivation to read showed greatly improved reading habits and attitudes using the Accelerated Reader. "Summary of Independent and Institute Research: Reading the Effectiveness of School Renaissance." Institute for Academic Excellence, Advantage Learning System, October 1, 1999.
2. Vollards, Topping, and Evans found that in two independent project designs, students using the Accelerated Reader Program had higher scores in reading comprehension. "Summary of Independent and Institute Research." Institute for Academic Excellence.
3. Peak and Dewalt five-year study found that Accelerated Reader students showed improved reading attitudes and higher reading scores on the California Achievement Test. "Summary of Independent and Institute Research." Institute for Academic Excellence.

BUILDING LEVEL ADMINISTRATIVE STAFFING

1. The organizational structures recommended in the High Schools That Work program require continuous involvement of school administration in planning strategies to achieve the key practices. www.nwrel.org/scpd/natspec/catalog/hsthatwork.htm.

2. School staffing ratios for all building-level administrative staff based on student enrollment and size of school district:

    Large School Systems (25,0000 or more pupils)
    50th Percentile   380.9
    10th Percentile   306.8
    Medium School systems (10,000–24,999 pupils)
    50th Percentile   392.8
    10th Percentile   300.6
    Small School Systems (2,500–9,999 pupils)
    50th Percentile   386.6
    10th Percentile   291.9
    Very Small School Systems (300–2,499 pupils)
    50th Percentile   327.4
    10th Percentile   223.5
    School Staffing Ratios—1997–1998. Education Research Service. Arlington, Virg. 1998.

CAREER CLUSTERS

1. "U.S. Department of Education has established 16 career clusters . . . clusters provide an ideal organizing tool to assist educators, counselors and parents in their work with students to identify their interests and goals for the future." Career Clusters, Office of Vocational and Adult Education. www.ed.gov/offices/OVAE/clusters.

2. "An important assumption is that some form of clustering of occupations and industries is a prerequisite for standards to become powerful tools in education reform and to strengthen workforce development in our country." "Standards: Making Them Useful—Occupational Clusters, Career Majors, and Programs." U.S. Department of Education. www.ed.gov/pubs/standards/clusters.html.

COMMUNITY SERVICE LEARNING

1. Research indicates that community service projects can contribute to student learning and growth. Jeffery Anderson, "Ser-

vice Learning and Teacher Education." ERIC ED421481, August 1998. www.ed.gov/databases/ERIC-Digests/ed/421481.htm.

2.   Practitioners have found that service learning has many benefits including improved citizenship, increased sense of importance in the community and development of skills applicable to the real world of work. "Resource Bulletin: School to Work and Service Learning." The National School-to-Work Learning & Information Center, May 1996. www.stw.ed.gov/factsht/bull1296.htm.

COUNSELORS

1.   Current national average student counselor ratio in elementary and secondary schools is 513:1; more than twice the 250:1 ratio recommended by the American School Health Association and American Counseling Association. "Bradley Writes Clinton for More School Counselors." American Counseling Association, June 1999. www.counseling.org/ctonline/specialsection/lettertoClinton.htm.

2.   American Health Association and National Education Association endorsed the American Counseling Association of maximum student counselor ratio of 250:1. "ASCA Legislative Update." American School Counselors Association, February 2000. www.schoolcounselor.org/february_20001.htm.

3.   The North Central Commission on Schools establishes a standard as it relates to guidance services: the school provides guidance services at a ratio equivalent to one counselor for each 200 students. NCA Commission on Accreditation and School Improvement. www.nca.asu.edu/standard/cp/ps.adp.

DISCIPLINE CODES/ALTERNATIVE PLACEMENTS/DRESS CODES

1.   As a result of the Texas Safe Schools Act in 1995, which requires districts to remove violent students from regular classrooms and place them in an alternative education setting, the number of teachers reporting threats of violence to students was down 6 percent and to themselves was down 33 percent. Number of assaults on other students was down 10 percent. Volokh and Snell, "Strategies to Keep Schools Safe." Reason Public Policy Institute, January 1998. www.rppi.org/education/ps234.html.

2. In Seattle, a Washington principal reported that before the dress code requirement, students were "draggin', saggin' and laggin." After the dress code, demeanor improved 98 percent, truancy and tardiness decreased, and thefts dropped to zero. Volokh and Snell, "Strategies to Keep Schools Safe." Reason Public Policy Institute, January 1998. www.rppi.org/education/ps234.html.

3. Most preliminary findings on school uniform codes come from Long Beach, California, where studies have found that suspension decreased by 32 percent, school crime by 36 percent, fighting by 51 percent, and vandalism by 18 percent, and attendance increased. "Nearly One Quarter of All Public Schools Now Require Uniforms." *School Administrator News*, August 13, 2000. www.schooladministrator.net/previous-news-aug13-00.html.

4. "An Action Guide for Creating Safe and Drug Free Schools" recommends that all schools establish and enforce rules that clearly define appropriate and inappropriate behavior and include zero tolerance for drugs, weapons, gangs, and violence. "An Action Guide—Action Steps for Schools." U.S. Office of Education, September 1996. www.uncg.edu/edu/ericcass/violence/docs/safe/steps.htm.

5. There exists a consensus among educators that it is important to provide alternative services, including counseling and support services during any school suspension or expulsion. "An Action Guide—Alternative Education Programs for Expelled Students." U.S. Office of Education, September 1996. www.uncg.edu/edu/ericcass/violence/docs/safe/altersc.htm.

6. "A school discipline code that is fairly and consistently enforced is essential to a safe and orderly school environment." "AFT Lessons for Life: Elements of an Effective Discipline Strategy." American Federation of Teachers, September 1995. www.aft.org/lessons/two/elements.html.

EXTENDED INSTRUCTIONAL TIME

1. The U.S. Department of Education recommended summer school as a promising option for increasing learning time as schools move to end social promotion: ". . . recent reviews of research on summer school have also begun to cement the idea that high quality summer programs can make a difference." Harrington-

Lueker, "Summer Learners." *American School Board Journal*, March 2000. www.asbj.com/2000/03/0300coverstory.html.
2. The Commission of Time and Learning concluded . . . that in order to acquire necessary competencies, students need more learning time than students presently receive. Part L—The Extended Time for Learning and Longer School Year, Sec.10993. H. R. 6 Improving American Schools Act of 1994. U. S. Congress, 1994. www.ed.gov/legislation/ESEA/sec10993.html.

FACILITIES

1. Research and common sense indicate that without a minimum level of quality for school facility, student and teacher effectiveness can be negatively impacted." "What Has Created California's School Facilities Predicament?" EdSource OnLine, April 1998. www.edsource.org/pub_edfct_pred.html.

FULL-DAY KINDERGARTEN TEACHERS

1. After a review of the literature, Rothenberg found that research showed attendance in full-day kindergarten programs resulted in academic and social benefits in the primary grades. Rothenberg, "Full Day Kindergarten Programs." May 1995. www.ed.gov/databases/ERIC_Digests/ed382410.html.
2. Cryan in 1992 found a positive relationship between attendance in full day kindergarten and later school performance. Rothenberg, "Full Day Kindergarten Programs." May 1995. www.ed.gov/databases/ERIC_Digests/ed382410.html.
3. A study by Elicker and Mathur in 1997 found that children who attended full-day kindergarten programs were academically stronger than those who attended half-day programs. "3 Structural Issues: Program Hours, Including Full day, Versus Sessional Kindergarten." U.S. Office of Education, 1997. www.doe.tased.edu.au/ooe/publications/structural_issues3si.htm.
4. Research shows that participation in a full day kindergarten positively affects student success. "Department of Defense Education Activity: DODEA Enhances Early Childhood Education." U.S. Department of Defense, June 23, 1999. www.odedodea.edu/communications/news/kindergarten/newkinder.html.

HOMEWORK

1. National Parent Teacher Association and National Education Association recommend the following amounts of homework: K–3 should have twenty minutes per day; grades four–six should have twenty to forty minutes per day, and grades seven–twelve should have no more than two hours per day. Milbourne and Haury, "Helping Students with Homework in Science and Math." *Clearinghouse for Science, Mathematics and Environmental Education,* May 1999. www.ericse.org/digests/dse99-03.html.

2. Cooper developed homework policy recommendations based on a review of over 100 research articles: grades one–three should have fifteen minutes; grades four–six should have fifteen to forty-five minutes; grades seven-nine should have forty-five to seventy-five minutes and grades ten–twelve should have seven-five to one hundred twenty minutes. "Homework Research & Policy—A Review of the Literature." Research/Practice 2, no. 2., August 2001. http://carei.coled.umn.edu/Rpractice/summer94/homework.htm.

MUSIC/ART INSTRUCTORS

1. Music is a vehicle to higher brain function. "Mozart Effect Controversy Continues." *AMC News,* August 24, 1999. www.geocities.com/Athens/2405/mozarteffect.html.

2. A survey conducted by the Gallup organization found that "more than nine in ten Americans believe music education should be part of every students day." "Music Making and Our Schools." AMC, 1998. www.amc-music.org/os/gallup.html.

3. National Standards for Music Education recommend that: (a) in grades Kindergarten–four "music is a basic expression of human culture, every student should have access to a balanced, comprehensive and sequential program of study in music;" (b) in grades five-eight that music instruction is particularly critical to the student's musical development; and (c) in grades nine–twelve the study of music contributes in important ways to the quality of each students' life. "K–12 National Standards, Pre-K Standards, and What They Mean to Music Educators." Music Educators National Conference, 1994. www.menc.org/publication/books/prek12st.html.

4. "Knowing and practicing the arts discipline are fundamental to the healthy development of children's minds an spirits . . . arts are inseparable from the meaning of the term education." "Summary Student—Education Reform Standards and the Arts." National Standards for Arts Education. MENC Publications, 1994. www.ed.gov/pubs/artsstandards.html.

5. John Goodlad maintains that arts are "one of the five givers of human knowledge, along with mathematics and science, literature and language, society and social studies, and vocations." Ernest Boyer offers "aesthetic literacy is as basic as linguistic literacy." "Why is Music Basic: The Value of Music Education." Music Rocks, June 1997. http://elwood.pionet.net/~hub7/value.htm.

PARENT INVOLVEMENT, PARENT CONTRACTS AND HOME VISITATION

1. Parent involvement significantly contributes to student learning. Buttery and Anderson, "Community School and Parent Dynamics—A Synthesis of Literature and Activities." ERIC #ED408244, 1997. www.kidscanlearn.com/learnpro/readprob/schl-par.html.

2. Caplan concludes that high levels of parent involvement have positive impact on attendance, drop-out rates, disciplinary problems, student motivation, and self-esteem. Caplan, "Parent Involvement 101: A Guide for Rural Educators." Rural Development Outreach Project, 1995. www.kidscanlearn.com/learnpro/readprob/schl-par.html.

3. Walberg found reading comprehension scores significantly improved for students in grades one–six whose parents signed a home school contract to assist students by providing a place to study; encouraging discussions each day, and attending progress meetings at the school. Gillum found that in three Michigan school districts where performance contracts with parents were used, greater gains in reaching achievement occurred. Flood, "The Relationship Between Parent Involvement and Student Achievement: A Review of the Literature." ERIC #ED357848, March 1993. www.uncg.edu/edu/ericcass/achieve/docs/ed357848.htm.

4. Based on numerous research studies, Christenson recommends numerous home school partnership programs that are designed to improve children success in school, such as home visitation,

parent involvement in learning, and parent contract programs. Christenson, "Home School Collaboration—Building Effective Parent-School Partnerships." University of Minnesota, 1993. www.cyfc.umn.edu/Learn/home.html.

3.   "Research shows that parent involvement improves student achievement." Arex, "Parent Involvement in Middle School Language Arts." ERIC Clearinghouse, June 1996. www.indiana. edu/%7eeeric_rec/ieo/digests/d115.html.

PRESCHOOL PROGRAMS

1.   All children, particularly those children who are at risk for reading difficulties, should have available early childhood education programs. Snow, Burns, Griffin, eds. "Preventing Reading Difficulties in Young Children." National Research Council, 1998. http://stills.nap.edu/html/prdyc/ch10.html.

2.   President Clinton, in the State of the Union address in 1999, stressed the importance of establishing preschool programs. www.whitehouse.gov/wht/sotu98/address.html.

READING RECOVERY/ONE-ON-ONE READING INSTRUCTION

1.   Nearly all the documents in the ERIC database found Reading Recovery program effective and recommend the program with only minor adjustments. Roger Sensenbaugh, "Reading Recovery." ERIC Clearinghouse, 1995. www.ed.gov/databases/ERIC_Digests/ed386713.html.

2.   "Children who are at risk for reading difficulties should be identified as soon as possible . . . . Additional instructional services in supplemental reading programs should be provided in first grade . . . . Instruction should be provided by a well qualified reading specialist . . . ." Snow, Burns, Griffin, eds. "Preventing Reading Difficulties in Young Children." National Research Council, 1998. http://stills.nap.edu/html/prdyc/ch10.html.

3.   "Studies have consistently shown that students served in Reading Recovery programs show significant increases in reading and writing with a high percentage (80 percent and higher) of children performing at or above average." Swartz, "California Early

Literacy Learning and Reading Recovery." California State University, 1998. www.stanswartz.com/cell_rr.htm.

READING SPECIALIST

1. All children should receive excellent reading instruction and children who are struggling with reading should receive additional instruction from professionals specifically prepared to teach them. Reading specialists who can provide expert instruction, evaluation and management for reading programs should be assigned to schools. A position statement: Teaching All Children to Read: The Roles of the Reading Specialist. International Reading Association, 2000. www.reading.org/advocacy/policies/specialist.html.
2. Every school should have access to specialists, including . . . reading specialist who have specialized training related to addressing reading difficulties and who can give guidance to classroom teachers." Snow, Burns, Griffin, eds. "Preventing Reading Difficulties in Young Children." National Research Council, 1998. http://stills.nap.edu/html/prdyc/ch10.html.
3. "Every child deserves excellent reading teachers because teachers make a difference in children's reading achievement and motivation to read" according to Carol M. Santa, president of the International Reading Association. International Reading Association, March 27, 2000. www.reading.org/advocacy/press_ 00327.html.

SCHOOL NURSES

1. National Association of School Nurses establishes a ratio of one nurse to 750 regular education students and one nurse to 250 special education students. Position Statement—Caseloads." National Association of School Nurses, June 1995. www.nasn.org/positions/caseload.htm.

SCHOOL PSYCHOLOGISTS

1. The new demand has resulted in school systems that can't find enough psychologists . . . Greater recognition of the important

roles that school psychologists play is prompting districts to create additional slots for these professionals." *Monitor on Psychology*, 31, no. 8., September 2000. www.apa/org/monitor/sep00/schoolpsych.html.

2. As school systems face more difficult challenges and psychologists are needed to assist students, administrators, and the community readily recognize that psychologists are invaluable resources. They assist students, teachers, administrators, and parents with meeting the challenges of the multitude of crises that disrupt the educational process. *Monitor on Psychology 31*, no. 8., September 2000. www.apa.org/monitor/sep00/school psych.html.

SCHOOL SECRETARIES/CLERKS

1. In New York City, an organized campaign to address the shortage of secretarial assistance in schools resulted in 1000 United Federation of Teacher members protesting to hire more secretaries. "Back to School 2000." *PSRP Reporter,* Fall 2000. www.aft.org/publications/psrp_reporter/fall2000nysecretaries.html.

2. *Education World* recently asked principals what would make their jobs more manageable. Principals response included the need for higher pay for school secretaries and the designation of at least one secretary as office manager. "From the Principal Files: The Principal Shortage—What Can Schools Do to Attract a New Generation of School Leaders?" *Education World,* November 1, 2000. www.educationworld.com/a_admin/admin197as.html.

SCHOOL SIZE

1. ". . . Smaller schools are more likely to become 'communities of learners' where everyone—students, parents, teachers, administrators and communities—feel they belong and have a sense of responsibility." Volokh and Snell, "Strategies to Keep Schools Safe." Reason Public Policy Institute, January 1998. www.rppi.org/education/ps234.html.

2. "Small schools encourage teachers to innovate and take ownership of the curriculum. Small school size improves student outcomes or grades and test cores . . . security improves and violence decreases." Klonsky, "Small Schools: The Numbers Tell the

Story." In Ernest Boyer, *The Basic School.* Carnegie Foundation, 1995, p. 211.

3.   "School size . . . was the key in the performance of students. Children do better in places small enough that the principal knows the name of each student." Johnson, "Study Says Small Schools Are Key to Learning." *The New York Times,* September 21, 1994, p. B 12.

4.   "Academic achievement in smaller schools is at least equal–and often superior–to that of larger schools." "School Improvement Research Series." North West Regional Educational Research Laboratory. www.nwrel.org/scpd/sirs/10/C020.html.

5.   A growing number of researchers are reporting that smaller schools are at least as important as smaller classes. "More studies have found that schools with low enrollments have better academic results, lower drop out rates and less student violence. "Researchers Build the Case for Smaller Schools." *The School Administrator News.* www.schooladministrator.net/previous-news-aug13-00.html.

SCHOOL SOCIAL WORKER

1.   The importance and necessity of school social work interventions has increasingly been recognized through legislative mandates. Education Commission Task Force NASW Standards for School Workers National Association of Social Workers, 1999. www.naswdc.org/practice/standards/school.htm.

2.   The National Council of State Consultants for Social Work Services has recommended school social worker ratio based on the characteristics of the student population to be served. A ratio of 1:800 for a total school population with special education and poverty concentrations, and a ratio of 1:500 for a total school population with special education, poverty and minority concentrations. "NASW Standards for School Social Workers," Education Commission Task Force, National Association of Social Workers, 1999. www.naswdc.org/practice/standards/school.htm.

STAFF DEVELOPMENT

1.   "Teachers require on-going in-service staff development support . . . . Professional development should not be conceived as some-

thing that ends with graduation from a teacher prep program . . .
local education authorities and teacher education programs
should give teacher support and skills throughout their careers."
Show, Burns, Griffin, eds., "Preventing Reading Difficulties in
Young Children." National Research Council, 1998. http://
stills.nap.edu/html/prdyc/ch10.html.

2.   "Lack of non-instructional time may be one of the chief reasons
our elementary schools have failed to emerge as institutions
ready for the 21st century." Purnell and Hill, *Time for Reform*.
Rand Corporation, 1992, p. 218.

3.   ". . . teachers need regular sustained time for staff development."
H.R. 6, Improving American's Schools Act of 1994, Part L, The
Extended Time for Learning and Longer Year. www.ed.gov/
legislation/ESEA/sec10993.html.

STANDARDS, HIGH EXPECTATIONS, AND MINIMUM SKILL REQUIREMENTS

1.   "Grade by grade standards are essential for parents and teachers." Jones, "The Standards Movement—Past and Present."
P.R.E.S.S., October 1996. www.execpc.com/~presswis/stndmvt.
html.

2.   "Standards provide for consistency in what student must know."
Kuhlman, "The Standards Reform Movement in the U.S." *TESOL
Matters*, 9, no. 5, October/November, 1999. www.tesol.
org/pubs/articles/tm9910-05.html.

3.   "Setting standards is important and also needs to be related to
work based preparation programs, performance based assessment and professional development." Anada, Rabinowitz, Caro-
los, and Yamashiro, "Skills for Tomorrow's Workforce." *West Ed
Policy Briefs*, 1995. www.wested.org/policy/pubs/full_text/
pb_ft_skills.htm.

4.   The report from the panel on National Education Goals establishes an expectation that schools will expect all students to
achieve at high levels. "Bringing All Students to High Standards," Report of the National Education Goal Panel. National
Education Goals Panel, 1990. www.negp.gov.

TEACHER CONTRACT PERIODS

1. A state-wide poll conducted by the Connecticut Education Association showed the majority of teachers favored extending their contract by one week for professional development. "Teachers Take Charge of Their Learning." *NEA News and Publications*, 1996. www.nfie.org/publications/charge/section2.htm.
2. National Association of Secondary School Principals calls for extending teacher contracts. 1996. www.nfie.org/publications/charge/section2.htm.
3. National Education Association recommends extending teachers contracts for up to four weeks for professional development that includes sustained study during the summer and follow-up training during the year. www.nfie.org/publications/charge/section2.htm.

TEACHER PAY

1. The 20th Century Fund has recommended federal government raise teacher salaries to a level of other professionals with similar schooling. Cooper, "Teacher Pay Raise Urged." *Washington Post*, August 13, 2000. www.washingtonpost.com/wp-dyn/articles/A21105-2000Aug13.html.
2. "Compensation is a potentially powerful tool that could be used to support education reform efforts, reward excellence and under grid a climate of educational excellence." "Reinventing Teacher Compensation Systems—1995." CPRE Policy Brief, September 1995. www.ed.gov/pubs/CPRE/fb6/fb6f.html.
3. Since 1975 teacher pay raises have grown less than the rate of inflation . . . increases have been inadequate to attract women to teaching profession since more professions are now welcoming women . . . . "All told we can't expect teachers' pay gains since 1965 to produce higher student achievement, for this result we would need bigger pay boosts to attract high quality college graduates to teaching." Rothstein, "The Myth of School Failure." American Perspectives OnLine, Spring 1993. www.prospect.org/archives/13/13roth.html.

TEACHERS—STUDENT/TEACHER RATIOS

1. President Clinton's 1998 State of the Union address placed strong emphasis on reduction of class size in the primary grades and requested funds for 100,000 teachers to reduce class size to eighteen. www.whitehouse.gov/WH/SOTU98/address.html.

2. Project STAR study found that students in reduced class size made statistically and educationally significantly greater gains than other students. Folger and Brenda, "Evidence from Project STAR About Class Size & Student Achievement. *Peabody Journal of Education 67*, 1:17–33, 1997. www.trochim.human.cornell. edu/tutorial/hussain/project.htm.

3. California Senate Office Research Legislative study found that in the early grades achievement of students in instructional groups of fifteen and fewer were 7 percentile ranks above that of students in classes of twenty-five to thirty. www.sen.ca.gov/sor/pubbysub.htm#education.

4. Research finds that students enrolled in smaller classes in grades K–3 do better academically. Hymon, "A Lesson in Classroom Size Reduction," ERIC Clearinghouse, July 1997. www.eric.uoregon.edu/trends_issues/organization/selected_ab stracts/evaluation.html.

5. ". . . students in reduced size classes had higher standardized test scores in math and reading." Eaglson, "Does Class Size Make a Difference? Recent Findings from State and District Initiatives." Office of Educational Research & Improvement, 1996. www.eric. uoregon.edu/trends_issues/organization/selected_abstracts/ evaluation.html.

6. ". . . report concluded that class size does impact student ratings of teacher effectiveness and course quality." Chiu, Wardrop, and Ryan, "Use of Unbalance Nested UNOVA to Examine the Relationship of Class Size to Student Ratings of Instructional Quality." EDRS, April 1999. www.eric.uoregon.edu/trends_issues/ organization/selected_abstracts/evaluation.html.

7. ". . . Research has established that smaller class size influences educational outcomes favorably." Achilees, Sharp, and Finn, "Pupil Teacher Ratio (PTR) and Class Size: What Is the Difference?" EDRS, November 1998. www.eric.uoregon.edu/trends_ issues/organization/selected_abstracts/evaluation.html.

8. The International Reading Association has endorsed efforts to reduce class size. "Summary of a Policy Resolution of the International Reading Association," May 1999. www.reading.org/ positions/class_size.html.

WELLNESS

1. "Over 6 million children are now considered obese, nutritionists warned educators that increasing amount of 'junk food' served in schools is hurting their efforts to get kids to eat healthier foods." "Nutritionists Warn of Increasing Junk Food Sales in Schools." School Administrator, October 2000. www.school administrator.net/previous-news-oct1-00.html.
2. American Academy of Pediatrics recommends that school increase physical activities in their curriculum. "Comprehensive, preferably daily, physical education for children in grades kindergarten through 12 is important." AAP Policy Statement 105, no. 5., May 2000. www.aap.org/policy/RE9907.html.
3. The President's Council on Physical Fitness and Sports Report recommends an increase in programs that enhance girls opportunities for participation in physical education and fitness programs. President's Council in Physical Fitness and Sports Report. U. S. Dept. of Health and Human Service, Spring 1997. http://education.umn.edu/tuckercenter/pcpfs/default.html.

Kanawha County Schools Performance and Development Review

Employee Name_____

Department/Division_____

Position Title (Superintendent, Deputy, Associate, Assistant Superintendent)_____

Date in Position_____

Immediate Supervisor_____

Review Covers Time Period_____

The purpose of the Performance and Development Review is to provide a systemic communication tool for managers and their employees to mutually define job expectations, evaluate and recognize performance, and help develop employees to their fullest potential.

KANAWHA COUNTY SCHOOLS PERFORMANCE SUMMARY

KEY BOARD OBJECTIVES

The Kanawha County School Board, in collaboration with the Superintendent, has identified thirteen (13) management objectives for the year 1995-96. Of the 13, five have been identified as key objectives, critical to the continuing success of the school system. The remaining objectives are also considered important and will be pursued to completion commensurate with available resources.

PERFORMANCE SUMMARY

Review performance on the job against each key element. Discuss results achieved, areas of success, and where improvements are needed. Cite examples where appropriate.

OBJECTIVE DESCRIPTION	COMMENTS

O-1 All schools will meet or exceed West Virginia State standards in the following indicators: Graduation Rate, Dropout Rate, Promotion/Retention, CTBS, Schools Effectiveness Inventory and Attendance

MO-2 To insure that all students will be prepared for the next level of education or the world of work as indicated by the four-year plan in place for each student, and that plan is reviewed with student, parent, and professional annually; college-bound enrollment, vocational placement, and college graduation.

MO-4 In regards to inclusion, to develop a process for reviewing student placement, resolving problems related to student placement, and improving communication with school system personnel, parents and the community.

MO-5 To establish alternative programs to provide basic instruction for students who are not successful in their home schools due to discipline problems or other behaviors that negatively impact their academic progress or the educational program of other students.

MO-12 To construct a balanced budget that reflects the mission and goals of Kanawha County Schools. To present a budget that defines program costs which meets the need of the Board in making allocation decisions.

OTHER OBJECTIVES

OTHER OBJECTIVES

OTHER OBJECTIVES

MOTHER MANAGEMENT OBJECTIVES	COMMENTS
MO-3 To improve teaching, learning, and productivity by expanding the use of technology by students.	
MO-6 To develop staff development programs that will enhance Kanawha County School employee effectiveness to result in improved student achievement.	
MO-7 To develop and implement a strategic plan for diversity program management that will improve human effectiveness and interaction in the school system.	
MO-8 To continue implementation of the established Comprehensive Communications/Telecommunications Plan.	
MO-9 To improve the learning climate in the classrooms and schools for students and the work environment for employees in Kanawha County Schools.	
MO-10 To complete the Blue Ribbon Plan for Education and for Facilities Consolidation, Expansion or Renovation.	

MO-11 To complete tasks as identified
from July 1, 1995, to June 30, 1996, for
Kanawha High School.

MO-13 To improve effectiveness of
Business Services by reducing cost to
$2,940,000/yr and by improving pro-
ductivity for an equivalent saving of
$520,000/yr.

OTHER OBJECTIVES

UNIVERSAL JOB ELEMENTS	PERFORMANCE SUMMARY/ COMMENTS
Knowledge of Work—Technical skills, experience, and knowledge required to perform the job. Is knowledgeable and up to date in curriculum and instructional trends and developments. Engages in activities to promote own professional growth and development.	
Quality of Work—Manner in which job is performed. Work is accurate, well-organized, timely, complete, and consistent. Prepares carefully for meetings.	
Contribution to Team Effort—Works cooperatively with others. Decisions and actions promote the success of the organization and the individual.	
Planning & Organizing—The ability to plan ahead, organize job tasks and activities, and make efficient use of time. Is effective in short- and long-range planning. Knows how to pace self.	

Communication—The ability to present and express information in an organized, understandable, complete, and concise manner . . . the ability to persuade or influence others through oral/written presentation. Keeps management fully informed about school operations.

Interpersonal Relations—The ability to interact effectively with others regardless of their level . . . the ability to develop rapport, trust and respect, as well as to accept work through interpersonal differences . . . promotes internal customer satisfaction.

Support of Kanawha County Vision, Mission, & Goals—Demonstrates potential to move system toward its vision, mission and goals. Adjust to changes in Board and the possible adjust by the Board in the vision, mission, and goals.

Implementation of School/System Policies—Supports management policy to public and staff. Maintains liaison between Board and personnel. Refrains from criticizing individuals or group members of the management team. Fully implements policy.

Support of School/System Policy Development—Superintendent supports Board as needed on new policies and procedures. Maintains position based on principle without regard to popularity until decision is reached, and then gives active support of decision.

Response to Management Request—
Provides ample information in a
timely fashion to enable management
decisions. Answers questions
promptly and follows up all management requests.

**Intergovernmental and Public Rela-
tions—**Maintains good relations with
local government leaders. Effectively
works with other agencies as required.
Handles media skillfully.

**School Law and Regulatory
Policies—**Possesses the knowledge
and understanding of how these areas
impact the job . . . ensures that all
operational and record-keeping tasks
are performed in accordance with
established policies and regulatory
requirements.

ADDITIONAL JOB ELEMENTS

ADDITIONAL JOB ELEMENTS

ADDITIONAL JOB ELEMENTS

ADDITIONAL JOB ELEMENTS

ADDITIONAL JOB ELEMENTS

MANAGERIAL JOB ELEMENTS	PERFORMANCE SUMMARY

Leadership—The ability to motivate,
support, inspire, and gain the respect
and confidence of subordinates. Leads
by example.

Direction—The ability to establish priorities, set goals, and then manage and
coordinate the available resources to
effectively and economically achieve
end results.

Follow-Up & Control—The ability to delegate responsibilities, monitor progress, and adjust priorities and resources in response to changing circumstances.

Development of Subordinates—The ability to effectively train, counsel, and evaluate the performance of subordinates. Involves staff members in board meetings. Effectively implements personnel evaluations.

SUMMARY COMMENTS

Provide a concise summary of this employee's performance. Your comments are critical in ensuring a rational and consistent basis for personnel and salary actions.

_____

_____

_____

_____

_____

_____

_____

I have reviewed this appraisal and discussed the contents with my supervisor. My signature means that I have been advised of my performance, but does not necessarily imply that I agree with the review or its contents. Use space below for comments.

_____

_____

_____

Signer_____Date_____

_____

APPROVALS

Supervisor's Signature_____ Date_____
Reviewed and Endorsed by _____ Date_____

FOR SUPERINTENDENT ONLY

Board President_____ Date_____
Board Member_____ Date_____
Board Member_____ Date_____
Board Member_____ Date_____
Board Member_____ Date_____

PERFORMANCE DEVELOPMENT PLAN
(PRESENT POSITION)

Areas for Development—Include
additional knowledge and skills to be
learned as well as behaviors and
styles that may need to be developed.

Action—List steps which can and will
be taken to address these development needs. Identify specific train-
ing/education/development
programs, if applicable.

CAREER PLANNING (FUTURE OPPORTUNITIES)

EMPLOYEE'S STATED
INTERESTS
AND ASPIRATIONS

Areas for Development—Include
knowledge and skills to be learned as
well as behaviors and styles that may
be needed for future positions.

Action—List steps which can and
will be taken to support realistic
career aspiration. Identify specific
training/education/development
programs, if applicable.

Kanawha County Schools Effective Schools Inventory

STUDENT QUESTIONNAIRE

DIRECTIONS: The following questionnaire is being done to get your opinions about your school. Please carefully read each of the following sentences. Think about how the statement describes your school. Next, choose the letter that matches how you feel.

A. Agree (This sentence describes my school most of the time.)

B. Sometimes (This sentence describes my school sometimes.)

C. Disagree (This sentence does *not* describe my school.)

D. I don't know

MARK your answers on the answer sheet provided. Use only a #2 PENCIL. Please note that there is a section on the answer sheet for you to make general comments about the strengths and weaknesses you feel exist at the school.

PART I: CLEAR AND FOCUSED MISSION

1. The main concern of the teachers and principal is helping students achieve.
2. I know what goals have been set to try to improve this school.
3. The teachers and principal work hard to make this a better school.

PART II: POSITIVE SCHOOL CLIMATE

4. This school is kept clean.
5. Things in this school that are broken get repaired very quickly.
6. This school is a bright, cheerful-looking place for students.

7.   There are clear rules for how students are to behave at school.
8.   Students behave well in the hallways and at lunch.
9.   Students feel that discipline in this school is fair.
10. Almost no students use drugs or alcohol on school grounds.
11. Almost no students use tobacco on school grounds.
12. Student bad behavior rarely interrupts my classes.
13. When a student breaks a rule, something is done about it.
14. Most students think that their classes are interesting.
15. My teachers seem enthusiastic about the subjects they are teaching.
16. Students are proud of going to this school.
17. The principal and teachers seem proud of working in this school.
18. The teachers seem to cooperate and help each other.
19. In class, we are taught how to work in small groups or in teams.
20. When my teachers give directions for homework or class assignments, I almost always understand them.
21. If I have a problem and need to see a teacher or other staff member, they make time for me.
22. Students are kept well-informed about activities going on in the school.
23. The teachers and principal seem to care a lot about the students.

PART III: STRONG INSTRUCTIONAL LEADERSHIP

24. The principal and teachers are leading activities to improve the school.
25. The staff seems to consider student ideas as they work to improve the school.
26. My teachers are knowledgeable about their subjects and how to teach them.
27. The principal is a good leader and works hard to improve the school.
28. If I need to see the principal or vice principal, he/she makes time for me.
29. I often see the principal throughout the school and in my classes.
30. Overall, this school seems to be well-organized and well-run.

PART IV: HIGH EXPECTATIONS FOR SUCCESS

31. This school seems to have good materials and equipment for teaching students.

32.   The principal and teachers expect a lot from students.
33.   The teachers and principal care about ALL the students, not just some of them.
34.   My teachers make students feel as though they can all learn.
35.   My teachers are clear about what must be done to pass their classes.
36.   My teachers try a variety of teaching methods to help all students understand the lesson.
37.   All teachers expect students to participate in class and complete their homework.
38.   Students who work hard to do well are recognized and rewarded.
39.   The teachers and principal are good role models for students.

PART V: TIME AND OPPORTUNITY TO LEARN

40.   Before beginning a lesson, my teachers let us know what we are supposed to learn from it.
41.   Teachers stress the importance of speaking and writing correctly.
42.   I feel that I am a good reader and writer.
43.   I feel that I have good skills in math.
44.   It is very difficult to get out of class without a good reason.
45.   Very little time is wasted in my classes.
46.   There are very few outside interruptions to my classes.
47.   Teachers do not allow student bad behavior to interrupt classes.
48.   If students need more time or extra help to learn something, my teachers arrange for it.
49.   In my classes, it is expected that everyone participates and everyone pays attention.
50.   My teachers use many different kinds of activities to keep the work interesting.
51.   I feel that I have good learning skills, like how to study, take notes, get organized, and so on.

PART VI: FREQENT MONITORING

52.   During class, teachers check often to make sure that students are understanding the lesson.
53.   We have quizzes and tests frequently to see how we are doing.
54.   We get tests and homework back very soon after we turn them in.

55. I feel that I am kept well informed about what grades I am getting in my classes.
56. If many students fail something on a test, my teachers go back and teach the information again.
57. I am rarely surprised about things on a test because it matches what we've covered in class.

PART VII: HOME/SCHOOL RELATIONS

58. I think that the teachers and principal like to have parents help in this school.
59. Parents and community support this school.

PART VIII: SCHOOL SATISFACTION

Overall, I am satisfied with my school.
Thank you for helping our school to improve!

PROFESSIONAL STAFF QUESTIONNAIRE

DIRECTIONS: The following questionnaire is designed to gather professional staff's perceptions about the school. It is organized around the seven correlates of an effective school.

Please carefully read each of the statements. Consider how accurately this accurately this statement describes your school. Choose the response that matches your general opinion of how the school operates, then MARK the appropriate box on the answer sheet. Use only a #2 PENCIL. The responses are as follows:
A. Agree (This is generally a strength at the school.)
B. Neutral (This is neither a strength nor weakness.)
C. Disagree (This is generally a weakness at the school.)
D. I do not have enough information to form an opinion.

Please note that there is a section on the answer sheet for you to make general comments about the strengths and weaknesses you feel exist at the school.

PART I: CLEAR AND FOCUSED MISSION

1. Our school has adopted a mission and a clear set of goals.

2. The staff believes that student achievement is the first priority of the school.
3. Virtually all staff understands the school's mission and goals.
4. Virtually all staff is committed to achieve the mission and goals for the school.
5. The mission and goals are the basis on which resources are allocated and decisions are made.
6. The school has an effective school improvement process in place.
7. Most staff members are actively involved in important activities derived from the School Improvement Plan.

PART II: POSITIVE LEARNING CLIMATE

8. The school is kept clean and well-maintained.
9. The school is attractive and inviting to students.
10. Students are orderly and well-behaved in the hallways and at lunch.
11. Students treat staff in a respectful manner.
12. Drug and alcohol use is not a problem in this school.
13. Vandalism is not a problem in this school.
14. The school discipline program is developmental and helps students learn to behave appropriately.
15. Student discipline procedures are consistent and fair.
16. Students seem enthusiastic about the learning process.
17. Teachers seem enthusiastic about teaching.
18. Students are proud and supportive of this school.
19. The staff is proud and supportive of this school.
20. The morale in this school is positive.
21. The staff seems optimistic about finding solutions to school problems.
22. There is a high level of trust and collaboration among the staff.
23. Student welfare is consistently the primary concern of the staff.

PART III: STRONG INSTRUCTIONAL LEADERSHIP

26. There is a clear sense of direction in this school.
27. There is focused leadership to improve curriculum and instruction.

28.   Virtually all teachers seem to have considerable knowledge of effective instruction.

29.   There is a school-wide emphasis on effective lesson design, including daily focused objectives, appropriate and varied activities, and good evaluation.

30.   The principal demonstrates expertise in curriculum and instruction.

31.   There is an on-going process for increasing staff knowledge of effective schooling and effective teaching.

32.   The school's resources are efficiently managed.

33.   The staff feels involved in the major decisions that affect the school.

34.   The principal is visible and accessible to staff and students.

35.   The principal organizes efficient procedures for managing school routines.

36.   The principal observes teachers and provides specific feedback regarding instructional practices.

37.   The staff evaluation process is effective in improving staff performance.

38.   The staff is proactive in securing additional resources for the school.

39.   Faculty Senate initiates activities that improve the overall operation of the school.

PART IV: HIGH EXPECTATIONS

40.   In this school, no student is treated better because of who they are.

41.   There is no overall dedication to excellence in this school.

42.   There is a sense of confidence among staff that they can teach just about any child that comes to his school.

43.   In this school, there is a consistent set of standards across like subjects and grades to determine if students pass.

44.   The staff sets high standards for students and is committed to helping students meet those standards.

45.   There is a school-wide emphasis on using teaching techniques that encourage all students to participate and be accountable.

46.   School procedures such as scheduling, teacher assignments, incentive programs, and so on are organized to address the needs of all students.

47.   Virtually all staff members in this school set very high standards for themselves.

PART V: OPPORTUNITY TO LEARN/TIME ON TASK

48.   There is a set of essential skills identified and taught for each subject and grade.
49.   There are effective procedures among elementary, middle/junior high, and high schools to coordinate curriculum and instruction.
50.   Within this school, there are effective procedures for articulating curriculum among subjects and grade levels.
51.   Virtually all students in this school have achieved mastery of basic-level skills.
52.   There are adequate programs and activities to remediate students who have not mastered basic grade-level skills.
53.   There are few outside interruptions that disturb classroom instruction.
54.   Classroom instruction is rarely interrupted by student misbehavior.
55.   School schedules are created so that students who need more time to learn are provided it.
56.   There is a school-wide emphasis on re-teaching information when students fail to master it.
57.   There is a school-wide emphasis on using teaching strategies that require students to actively participate in the instructional process.
58.   There is a school-wide emphasis on using instructional strategies that address different learning styles and modalities.
59.   Students have effective learning skills like how to study, take notes, get organized, and so on.

PART VI: FREQENT MONITORING

60.   Teachers seem to be familiar with a variety of techniques that can be used to check for student understanding during a lesson.
61.   In this school, there seems to be a variety of procedures (besides paper and pencil tests) used to formally assess student mastery.

62. Student evaluation procedures used in this school seem to assess higher-order thinking processes as well as memorization of facts.
63. Students seem to be kept well-informed about how they are doing in their classes.
64. Classroom test results seem to be used as much for remediation and enrichment purposes as for giving students a grade.
65. The concept of curriculum alignment is understood and used by teachers in this school.
66. Norm-referenced testing such as CTBS aligns with the curriculum in this school.
67. There is an effective school-wide process for using CTBS test results to improve curriculum and instruction.
68. Across the same subjects and grades, teacher-made tests assess the same concepts.
69. The staff uses CTBS scores and other student data to improve curriculum and instruction.
70. Data area collected and used to evaluate the effectiveness of extracurricular programs.

PART VII: HOME/SCHOOL RELATIONS

71. The staff does a variety of things to encourage parent involvement in the school.
72. There are many parent volunteer programs that enhance student achievement.
73. There is considerable community support for the school and its programs.
74. Parents seem to know specific ways that they can help students do better at school.
75. Parent opinion is respected and considered when school issues are addressed.
76. The school's procedures for communicating with parents are effective.
77. There are adequate opportunities for parent/teacher conferences.
78. There are effective processes for involving parents in school decisions.

PART VIII: SCHOOL SATISFACTION

79. Overall, I am satisfied with this school.

Thank you for working to make this school a better place for students.

SERVICE PERSONNEL QUESTIONNAIRE

DIRECTIONS: The following questionnaire is designed to gather service personnel's opinions about their school. The questionnaire is organized around the seven areas that research has shown to be present in an effective school.

Please carefully read each of the statements. Think how this statement describes your school. Reply to the statements in the following way:

A. Agree (This is generally a strength at the school.)

B. Neutral (This is neither a strength nor weakness.)

C. Disagree (This is generally a weakness at the school.)

D. I do not have enough information to form an opinion.

MARK your answers on the answer sheet using a #2 PENCIL. Your responses should apply ONLY to your SCHOOL, NOT to other schools you have worked in or other schools you know about. Please note there is a section on the answer sheet for you to make general comments about the strengths and weaknesses you feel exist at the school.

PART I: CLEAR AND FOCUSED MISSION

1. I can tell from their actions and discussions that the staff puts student learning first.
2. I know about the school's mission and goals for improvement.
3. Service personnel are involved in activities to improve the school.
4. The staff seems committed to working on activities that are included in the School Improvement Plan.

PART II: POSITIVE SCHOOL CLIMATE

5. The building is kept clean.
6. When things are broken, they get fixed quickly.
7. Improvements are made to the school to make it an attractive place for students to learn.
8. Students are orderly and well-behaved.
9. Students are respectful to service personnel.
10. Alcohol and rug use is not a problem in this school.

11. Tobacco use by students on school grounds is not a problem.
12. When students break the rules, something is done about it.
13. When students break the rules, they seem to be treated fairly.
14. Students seem to be enthusiastic about learning.
15. The teachers and principal seem to be enthusiastic about their work.
16. Students act as though they are proud of going to this school.
17. The service personnel seem proud to be working in this school.
18. The staff has a positive attitude about working in the school.
19. The teachers and service personnel get along well and support each other.
20. Service personnel are made to feel that they are important to the school's success.
21. There is good communication between service personnel and teachers.
22. There is good communication between service personnel and the principal.
23. What's good for students is the first concern of the teachers and principal.
24. Helping the school to be a better place for students is very important to service personnel.

PART III: STRONG INSTRUCTIONAL LEADERSHIP

25. The principal is a strong leader in helping the staff to make the school more effective.
26. The principal has good ideas on how to improve the school.
27. The school's money and other resources are seldom wasted.
28. It is easy to talk with the principal if you have a problem or concern.
29. This school runs smoothly and things seem well-organized.
30. The principal provides assistance to help service personnel improve their job skills.
31. Service personnel are evaluated according to guidelines.

PART IV: HIGH EXPECTATIONS

32. Students in this school know that they are expected to work hard at their schoolwork.
33. The staff acts as though they care equally about all students.

34.   The school staff works hard to find solutions to school problems.
35.   There are many activities and rewards that encourage students to do their best.
36.   The staff works hard and sets high standards for themselves.
37.   The principal set high standards for self and others.

PART V: OPPORTUNITY TO LEARN/TIME ON TASK

38.   It has been made clear that teachers are not to be interrupted or disturbed during class time.
39.   Students are not allowed out of class without a very good reason.

PART VI: FREQUENT MONITORING

(No items on this area)

PART VII: HOME/SCHOOL RELATIONS

40.   Parents are made to feel welcome when they come to the school.
41.   Parents are encouraged to volunteer time to help the school.

PART VIII: SCHOOL SATISFACTION

42.   Overall, I am satisfied with this school.

Thank you for helping our school to improve.

PARENT QUESTIONNAIRE

DIRECTIONS: The following questionnaire is designed to gather parents' opinions about their child's school. It is organized around the seven areas that research has shown to be present in effective school. Consider whether or not the statement describes the school named at the top of the answer sheet.
    Reply to the statements in the following way:
    A. Agree (This is generally a strength at the school.)
    B. Neutral (This is neither a strength nor weakness.)
    C. Disagree (This is generally a weakness at the school.)
    D. I do not have enough information to form an opinion.

MARK your answers on the answer sheet using a #2 PENCIL. Your responses should apply ONLY TO THE SCHOOL NAMED ON THIS FORM, NOT to other schools your child may have attended or other schools you know about. Please note there is a section on the answer sheet for you to make general comments about the strengths and weaknesses you feel exist at the school.

PART I: CLEAR AND FOCUSED MISSION

1. The school's main focus seems to be improving student achievement.
2. I am aware of the school's mission and goals for improvement.
3. Student achievement is the main concern when the school spends money or makes decisions.
4. This school has an on-going process for improving the school.
5. The staff seems committed to improving the school.

PART II: POSITIVE SCHOOL CLIMATE

6. The building is clean and well-maintained.
7. The building is an attractive and inviting place for learning.
8. Students are orderly, well-behaved, and respectful.
9. Discipline procedures are consistent and fair throughout the school.
10. The discipline procedures are designed to help students learn appropriate behavior.
11. Students seem enthusiastic about learning at this school.
12. The staff seems enthusiastic about learning at this school.
13. Students feel proud of going to this school.
14. Overall, the staff has a positive attitude about what they can do for students.
15. The staff communicates clearly to students about such things as rules, homework, and so on.
16. The welfare of students comes first with the staff in this school.

PART III: STRONG INSTRUCTIONAL LEADERSHIP

17. The principal provides strong leadership in improving the school.

18. The principal seems knowledgeable about how to make the school excellent.
19. My child's teachers seem to know their subjects and how to teach them.
20. The principal is available to parents to discuss ideas and concerns.
21. When I call or visit the school, the staff seems efficient and organized.
22. The school has an adequate supply of good-quality materials for teaching students.

PART IV: HIGH EXPECTATIONS FOR SUCCESS

23. The teachers set high standards for my child's work.
24. The staff acts as though they care equally about all students.
25. The teachers help my child to feel confident that he/she can learn.
26. The teachers and principal strive to find solutions to student problems.
27. Students are kept informed about what they must know to master their subjects.
28. The school provides effective programs that help children of all abilities to do well.
29. There are many activities and rewards that encourage students to do their best.
30. The teachers are good role models for hard work and high standards.
31. The principal is a good role model for hard work and high standards.

PART V: TIME AND OPPORTUNITY TO LEARN

32. Parents are made aware of the skills that students must know for each subject and or grade.
33. In this school, students do not pass on unless they master certain academic skills.
34. For the same subject and grade, students are expected to know the same skills regardless of the teacher.
35. The school stresses the importance of students mastering basic skills (reading, writing, speaking, and mathematics).

36.   Very little classroom time is wasted at my child's school.
37.   The school stresses that classroom time should not be inter-
        rupted.
38.   At school, arrangements are made to give students extra time
        when they need it to learn something.
39.   Teachers seem to teach in ways that my child is able to learn.
40.   My child has learned good study skills.

PART VI: FREQUENT MONITORING

41.   My child seems to be kept informed on how well he/she is doing
        in classes.
42.   I am kept well-informed about how my child is doing in classes.
43.   When my child does poorly on a test, help is provided so that
        he/she will understand the information before going on to a new
        lesson.
44.   Parents are provided data that shows overall how effective the
        school is.

PART VII: POSITIVE HOME/SCHOOL RELATIONS

45.   The staff makes parents feel welcome when they come to the
        school.
46.   Parents are encouraged to contact the school if they have a con-
        cern.
47.   Parents are encouraged to volunteer time to help the school.
48.   When a problem arises with students, parents feel that their opin-
        ions are important to the staff.
49.   The school has let me know of things to do to help my child be a
        better student.
50.   There is adequate time and opportunity for parent/teacher con-
        ferences.
51.   There is adequate communication between the school and the
        home.
52.   There is adequate communication between the between the
        teachers and the home.
53.   The school involves parents in making decisions about the
        school.

PART VIII: SCHOOL SATISFACTION

54.   Overall, I am satisfied with my child's school.

Thank you for helping our school to improve!

References

Adler, Mortimer. *Paideia Proposal*. New York: Macmillian, 1982.

Alvarado, Tony. "District #2 New York City School Improvement." Columbia University Superintendent Conference. Columbia University, New York, 11 (July 1997).

American School Counselors Association. "ASCA Legislative Update." February 2000. www.schoolcounselor.org/february/2000.htm.

Bottoms, Gene, Alice Presson, and Mary Johnson. *Making High Schools Work*. Atlanta: Southern Region Education Board, 1992.

Boyer, Ernest. *The Basic School—A Community for Learning*. Princeton, N.J.: Carnegie Foundation, 1995.

Browns, Ralph Emerson. *The New Dictionary of Thoughts*, rev. ed. Standard, 1963.

Business and Industrial Development Corporation. *Metro Charleston*. Charleston: BIDCO (Business and Industrial Development Corporation), 1999.

———. *Metro Charleston: The Gateway Region*. Charleston: BIDCO (Business and Industrial Development Corporation), 1996.

Carver, John. *Boards That Make a Difference*. San Francisco: Jossey-Bass, 1990.

Center on National Education Policy. *Do We Still Need Public Schools?* Bloomington, Ind.: Phi Delta Kappa, 1996.

Committee for Economic Development. *Putting Learning First*. New York Committee for Economic Development, 1994.

Covey, Steven. *First Things First*. New York: Simon and Schuster, 1994.

———. *The Seven Habits of Highly Effective People*. New York: Simon and Schuster, 1989.

Dianda, Marcella. *The Superintendent's Can-Do Guide to School Improvement*. Washington, D.C.: Council for Educational Development and Research, 1984.

Education Research Service. *School Staffing Ratios: 1997–1998*. Arlington, Va.: Education Research Service, 1998.

Elam, Stanley, ed. *The State of the Nation's Public Schools*. Bloomington, Ind.: Phi Delta Kappa, 1994.

Erlandson, David A., Peggy L. Stark, and Sharon M. Ward. *Organizational Oversight*. Princeton, N.J.: Eye on Education, 1996.

Eyre, Eric. "Alice Moore's Textbook Battle Shook Up School Board, County." *Charleston Gazette*, 23 May 1999.

Fields, Joseph C. *Total Quality for School: A Suggestion for American Education*. Milwaukee: ASQC Quality Press, 1993.

———. *Total Quality for Schools—A Guide for Implementation*. Milwaukee: ASQC Quality Press, 1994.

Freeman, Arthur, and Rose DeWolf. *Woulda, Coulda, Shoulda*. New York: Harper Collins, 1989.

Glickman, Carl D. *Revolutionizing American's Schools*. San Francisco: Jossey-Bass, 1998.

Harris, V. B. *Great Kanawha*. Charleston: Jarrett Printing, 1974.

Henderson, Nan, and Mike M. Milstein. *Resiliency in Schools*. Thousand Oaks, Calif.: Corwin Press, 1994.

Hodgkinson, Harold. "Why Have Americans Never Admired Their Own Schools?" *School Administrator* 53, no. 5 (May 1996).

Kanawha County Schools, ed. "Minimum Requirements," "School Profiles," *Kanawha County Schools Policy Manual*. Charleston, W.V.

Kaufman, Roger, and Douglas Zahn. *Quality Management Plus*. Newbury Park, Calif.: Sage Publishing, 1983.

Kentucky Department of Education. *Kentucky Education Reform*. Frankfort, Ky.: Kentucky State Department, 1995.

Kern, Jim. *Build the Fort Today*. San Antonio, Texas: Desktop Publishing Services, 1990.

Kincheloe, Joe L. *Understanding the New Right and Its Impact on Education*. Bloomington, Ind.: Phi Delta Kappa, 1983.

Lezotte, Lawrence W. *Correlates of Effective Schools: The First and Second Generation*. Okemos, Mich.: Effective School Products, 1991.

Lezotte, Lawrence W., and Beverly A. Bancroft. "Beyond Student Outcomes: Some Promising Side Effects of Using the Effective Schools Research Framework." *NYC Challenge*. New York: NYASCD, 1987.

McDonald, Joseph P. *Redesigning School-Lessons for the Twenty-first Century*. San Francisco: Jossey-Bass, 1996.

McKay, Jack. "The Forces Most Destructive of Public Education." *School Administrator* 53, no. 5 (May 1996).

Meir, D. "The Kindergarten Tradition in High School." *Progressive Education for the 1990's: Transforming Practice*, ed. K. Jervis and C. Montag. New York: Teachers College Press, 1991.

Morgan, Gareth. *Creative Organizational Theory*. Newbury, Calif.: Sage Publishing, 1989.

———. *Images of Organization*. Newbury, Calif.: Sage Publishing, 1986.

Morgan, John G., and Robert J. Byers. *Charleston 200*. Charleston: Charleston Gazette, 1994.

Neff, Jim. "MEA Insider." Michigan Education Association Region 15B Website, September 2001.

Nugent, Tim. *Death at Buffalo Creek*. New York: W. W. Norton, 1973.

Oswald, Lori Jo. "School Based Management." *ERIC Digest* 99 (July 1994).

———. "Work Teams in Schools." *ERIC Digest* 103 (February 1996).

Owens, Robert G. *Organizational Behavior in Education*. Englewood Cliffs, N.J.: Prentice Hall, 1991.

National Education Association. *Kanawha County, West Virginia: A Textbook Study in Conflict*. Washington, D.C., 1975.

National Education Commission on Time and Learning. *Prisoners of Time*. Washington, D.C.: U.S. Department of Education, 1994.

Patterson, Jerry. *Coming Clean about Organizational Change*. Arlington, Va.: American Association of School Administrators, 1997.

———. "Harsh Realities about Decentralized Decision Making." *School Administrator*, 55, no. 3 (March 1998).

Plumley, W., Marjorie Warner, and Lorena Anderson. *Things Appalachian*. Charleston: Morris Harvey College, 1976.

Reeves, Douglas B. "Holding Principals Accountable." *School Administrator*, 55, no. 9 (October 1998).

Reustle, Harry G. "Seven Habits of Highly Effective Financial Superintendents." Charleston: Kanawha County Schools, 1996.

Rice, Otis K. *West Virginia—A History*. Lexington, Ky: University Press, 1985.

Robinson, Glen, and David Brandon. *Perceptions about America Education: Are They Based on Facts?* Arlington, Va.: Educational Research Service, 1992.

Saukhanou, Anne, ed. *Webster's II New Revised Dictionary*. Boston: Houghton Mifflin, 1998.

Schlechty, Phillip C. *Inventing Better Schools*. San Francisco: Jossey-Bass, 1997.

Sergiovanni, Thomas J. *Building Community in Schools*. San Francisco: Jossey-Bass, 1994.

Shaw, Gordon, Frances Rauscher, Linda Levine, Eric Wright, Robert Newcomb. *Neurological Research*, Vol. 19 (February, 1997).

Silver, Lee. "Why I'm Giving Up on School Boards." *School Administrator*, 55, no. 2 (February 1998).

Steinberg, Laurence. *Beyond the Classroom*. New York: Simon and Schuster, 1996.

Thompson, James. "Systemic Education Reform." *ERIC Digest* 90 (May 1994).

Tomlinson, G., and Richard C. Wergen. *West Virginia Book of Lists*. Sutton, W.V.: MainStream Books, 1994.

U.S. Department of Commerce. "County and City Data Profile." Washington, D.C., 1994.

———. *Social and Economic Characteristics of West Virginia*. Washington, D.C., 1998.

———. *What Really Matters in American Education*. Washington, D.C., 1997.

Wallace, Richard C., and David Engle. *The Learning School*. Thousand Oaks, Calif.: Corwin Press, 1997.

Wasley, Patricia A., Robert L. Hampel and Richard W. Clark. *Kids and School Reform*. San Francisco: Jossey-Bass, 1997.

Williams, John Alexander. *West Virginia*. New York: W. W. Norton, 1984.

———. *West Virginia: A History for Beginners*. Charleston: Appalachian Editions, 1993.

Young, Ken. "A Plan for Becoming a Better School System." South Charleston: Marshall University Graduate College, 1995.

Index

About the Author

Jorea M. Marple is an educator who has worked in many positions during the past thirty years, including elementary school teacher; reading teacher; reading specialist; central office administrator in a variety of areas including special education, federal programs, special projects, and planning; principal; adjunct undergraduate and graduate instructor; and superintendent of schools. Marple has been recognized for accomplishments throughout her professional life. Her work as an elementary principal brought national recognition to an inner-city school, Tiskelwah Elementary, as a West Virginia Blue Ribbon School and National Blue Ribbon School; Tiskelwah Elementary was also selected by *Redbook Magazine's* as one of America's Best Schools. As superintendent of Kanawha County Schools Dr. Marple implemented a management plan that established higher standards and increased accountability and resulted in dramatically improved standardized test scores, administrative and fiscal management, and program development and expansion.

Marple received her Ed.D. in education administration from West Virginia University. She has received numerous honors and recognitions including the Presidential Award from West Virginia State College, the "Hats Off" Award from the National Council of Jewish Women, Superintendent of the Year from the West Virginia Music Association, and selected participant in the Superintendent's Academy at Columbia University and Harvard University.